The Gratitude Cloak

A Memoir

KATIE HAMMOND

Dedicated to Funky, Chunky and Monkey.

Gratitude changes everything.

CONTENTS

CHAPTER 1

There is a lyric in Baz Luhrmann's Sunscreen song about the real troubles in your life blindsiding you on 'some idle Tuesday'. Baz was right. Although not about the idle bit, because getting three small boys out of the door to school isn't exactly relaxing, but it was a Tuesday.

Josh had had a fever, no other symptoms, for a week. We were keeping it at bay with the usual paracetamol and ibuprofen, and as soon as they kicked in, he was a normal five year old for a couple of hours, before getting shiny-eyed and rosy-cheeked and creeping up to 39 degrees. On the third day I took him to the GP who prescribed antibiotics for a suspected sinus infection. Everything else was clear: chest, throat, no infected cuts or grazes... Forty-eight hours later I lie in bed with him at midnight holding a damp flannel on his forehead willing the paracetamol to kick in more quickly. My hand rests on his little chest and I can feel his heart absolutely hammering. Reach for the iphone... google 'five year old fever high heart rate'. Google reassures me that tachycardia is absolutely normal for a child fighting a fever, and also reminds me that fever is the body's natural way of fighting infection. I'll take him back to the GP in the morning.

Day 1

The GP looks concerned, does another thorough examination, prescribes a different stronger antibiotic and tells us to come back the following morning if he still has a fever tonight. He does, it rockets up to 40.1. Between damp flannels, doses of syrups and calming words, baby Albie wakes up and needs feeding back to sleep – he is eleven months old and is breastfed. Husband Scott is working away from home. I check on Ollie as I walk back to our bedroom; he is seven and as usual he is lying flat on his back on his top bunk, Cookie the seal next to his face, breathing soundlessly. He is the neat sleeper, Josh is the wriggler. Albie is a baby so doesn't get a label yet.

I lower myself back into my side of the bed next to hot Joshie and start feeling that slightly guilty mum feeling of concern muddled with vague annoyance that the gods of childhood illnesses are messing about with us. I'm already exhausted; Albie doesn't sleep through, and Scott is still building up his strength after a massive spinal surgery earlier in the year. It strikes me that we could do with a nice calm stretch. I lie in the dark thinking about how Scott is still recovering physically and mentally; he has just started trying to work out how to incorporate physio and rehab into his daily life, and he needs the space to make some psychological adjustments. I put that thought in a little drawer in my head and close it. Will have to come back to that later.

Scott's business is in Sydney, we live ninety minutes away, and like many people in our local community, he stays in the city a few nights a week. This means I am fairly used to being a solo parent with the three little boys, and it also means I have quickly formed gorgeous friendships with people who know I may sometimes tentatively call on them, and mums in the same boat. It is not ideal, and it is not the long term plan, but this is the compromise we made to live in a beautiful spot in our own more affordable home, and when we moved away from the city not so long ago one of the main reasons we gave was our longing, after living overseas for years, to belong to a local community. Well we certainly got that.

Back home with feverish Joshie, and the following morning is the first day back to school after the Spring holiday. Here in Australia this is the final term of the year, the term when the weather hots up towards Christmas (always weird, as a Brit) and the kids start to get really worn out. Ollie is in Year 1. Josh is in his final term of preschool, but only goes three days a week and today is not one of them. We drop Ollie at school and head back to the GP. She prescribes a different antibiotic but also suggests a blood test "just to rule out something more serious like glandular fever." I think, he's five, he hasn't snogged anyone yet. To my knowledge. Now I look back and think oh glandular fever, could it not have been you?

I trust this GP, she is brilliant and always sees the whole picture, looks at stuff in the context of the five of us not just individual patients, but I still ask tentatively if she really thinks sticking a needle in him is necessary. He is a calm, self-assured child but I will need to think fast and come up with a game plan if needles are involved. Both our older boys love to know what is happening and don't particularly like going off piste with their day. Also I'm not sure he has ever encountered a needle apart from for vaccinations, which they know give them a magic shield against horrible diseases. Yes, she explains, if he's had a temperature for seven days, if the antibiotics made no impact and if his fever is reaching 40, it's better to have a quick minute of discomfort so we can see exactly what is going on in the bloods. It'll give us a clear picture. All good, Albie smiles at me and Josh from his buggy, the GP writes a long list on the form of things she wants Pathology to test for, I smile with a feeling of 'excellent this is all going to be fine and we will have peace of mind', and we do the blood test. Josh stares hard at the needle going into his arm, stays pretty cool, I go into science mode (an unplanned technique which will serve me well) and explain that they can look at the blood under a microscope and see teeny tiny things in it which will tell them why he keeps getting hot, Albie sucks on a tiny rice cake, and we leave with stickers and a lollipop. If I sound sort of perfunctory and like a robot it's because at this point he was basically just normal Josh as soon as the paracetamol or ibuprofen kicked in, and only in the half hour between doses wearing off and the next dose taking effect was he in any way a sick child. Though even then it was literally just a fever, he didn't have any other symptoms. And knowing now what it was, it's also worth noting that he wasn't particularly pale and didn't have lots of unexplained bruises.

After we pick up Ollie from school later that day we swing by the newsagent to get a birthday card for a friend and on a whim I buy Josh a blue teddy bear for being so brave about his blood test. 'Blue Bear' is cuddled for a couple of hours and then left upside down under their bunk beds and I feel daft for being so soft – I think I bought it more for me. Well done me for having a middle child who is so easy going about blood tests, ha!

That night he is still hot, the new stronger antibiotic doesn't make a scrap of difference.

Day 2

8.50am Tuesday morning. Albie is strapped into his

removable car seat sitting by the front door, I am filling water bottles and shouting all those morning mum commands in various tones of stress which make me feel like I have become someone I am not.

"Shoes on! Library bag Ollie! Josh! Shoes on! Reader Ollie! Did we do your reader last night? Shhh-ugar we didn't no no we did it was about monkeys - Josh put them ON!" etc etc. I run back to the bedroom and shove my shoes on, and on the spur of the moment I also put on my new present which I bought for myself and a strung-out friend after reading the company's blog about how women really can handle the toughest of times - a stainless steel bangle stamped in functional capital letters with the words: 'YOU'VE GOT THIS'. Listening to the building little-boy mayhem near the front door I smile and shove it hastily on my wrist, this'll see me through the school run, stay cool and use a kind voice, you've got this! God I had so much energy.

Back to the front door and my phone rings. I glance at it, managing to think in less than a second my standard exasperated, 'For god's sake Scott why do you always ring to say good morning just as we are trying to get out of the door?!' This happens astonishingly often and can't be unique to this family. But it doesn't say 'Scott Awesome' it says 'No Caller ID'. The only times my phone has said 'No Caller ID' have been when I was pregnant and midwives would ring me to make exciting, happy appointments. I consider ignoring it and then something in me says, 'medical'. So I answer it.

A young, male voice in fluent Asian-accented English: "Aah is that the mother of Joshua Hammond?"
"Yes." I might need to hear what he says, he used Josh's full name, only official people do that. I step out of the back door and shut it so I can hear him, whilst waving

through the glass at the boys to stay put. Albie starts crying. I wave at Ollie to go to Albie. Ollie starts dancing right up in Albie's face like a possessed sprite. Josh shouts, "Mu-uummeee I need a weeeee…"

"Aah this is Chris from St Vincent's Children's Hospital Pathology Laboratory." Or something. "Did you order a blood test for Joshua Hammond?"

"Err, yes, we did one yesterday at the GP." This is weird and slightly irritating taking this call now. We are going to be late for school.

"Aah I have been trying to call your GP several times but her phone line is busy, so I am calling you as this is important. I have some concerns about Joshua's blood results. Some of the numbers they are really very low. Some cells are very, very low, almost zero. I think you need to take him straight to the doctor."

What a pain. Seriously? What on earth has Josh picked up? "Ok, err…so I should go to the GP this morning…?" I tail off.

"Aah I think you need to take him to the Emergency department of the hospital."

What? "Oh right, I see." I am calm, I feel nothing. Numb. The boys are now shouting at each other. How can kids feel drama brewing through a glass sliding door?

"Mrs Hammond what is your nearest hospital?"

Mrs Hammond, always sounds weird, albeit in a nice way. Like I should have proper big bosoms and be really capable and a real adult. I click into organizational mode, I like questions with straight answers. I tell him, then add, "We can be there in less than ten minutes."

"OK I will call your local hospital now and let them know you are coming in. I will also continue to try to reach your GP."

"Ok, thank you." He is calling ahead? Wobbly neon letters form in front of my vision: WT…?

I take a deep breath and step back into the house,

"Boys. Ok. Ollie grab your bag and library bag, Josh why haven't you done your wee in the loo yet, you know where it is – ok do your wee on the lemon tree, meet you at the gate. Let's go."

We set off down the driveway and out onto the main road. My mind is working out the logistics of the next couple of hours: school is literally on the way to the hospital and there is no point Ollie coming with us and waiting around in ER, we'll drop him first but he'll have to do kiss and drop. As I am about to suggest this to Ollie my phone rings through the car bluetooth. It's the GP. She sounds efficient and calm and very, very direct.

"Hello Katie, where are you right now?"

"I am driving with the three boys on the way to the hospital as I had a call from the Pathology lab telling me to do that, did they call you?"

"Yes. I am calling to let you know that you mustn't panic, you need to stay calm and drive safely to Emergency."

I see my knuckles on the steering wheel. They are starting to look a little bit white.

"OK. We are doing that. Thank you."

"Don't rush, but go straight there and I will talk to you later." She hangs up.

Ollie starts asking questions, Josh is silent, Albie is smiling at everyone.

"Now Joshie that was the doctor who has seen the blood test you did yesterday and she wants us to go to the hospital so they can check you are ok, so we'll just drop Ollie and then we'll go there."

Big pause.

"I. DO. NOT. WANT. TO. GO. TO. THE. HOSPITAL."

"It's the one where I had Albie and where Daddy did physio, it's a happy hospital with the nice sweets in the cafe, all the people who work there want to make everyone better."

Right, compartmentalize.

We reach school and I see a friend with a son in Ollie's class. I pull over and hand him over. She is a nurse, I know her well and would trust her with my life; I silently send a little thank you to the heavens for making it her who was standing there at that moment. I splurge something breathlessly about white cells and phonecalls. She later tells me when she heard the words 'white cells' she shivered. When I get back in the car I am in full crisis mode.

Josh now really does not want to go and starts protesting. I go through the various phases of persuasion: calm and kind, calm and firm, calm and strict, fake-teary (always works with my boys, but doesn't this time, he is scared understandably), silent and steely. We park and he goes mental. I unload Albie into his buggy and then do the full hands on hips, 'Right!' thing with Josh. I reach in to try and lift him out of the car. He braces himself against the doorframe. I prise his fingers, he yells… this goes on for a few minutes and finally, god knows how, I find the strength to manhandle him out of the car and sort of drag him under my arm, him shouting, "Well now you can't get inside the hospital because you can't take Albie's bugaboo up the STAIRS!"

Me, icy and quiet, "They have a ramp. Stop it."

"NOOOO!" Furious, all the way up the ramp. I think about how stereotypical we must look to an outsider: a frazzled mum with a baby dragging a little boy…blah blah…

The second we get to the Emergency doors he stops shouting. He is oddly self-conscious for a five year old and scared of being told off by anyone except me. Silent and sullen he stands behind my leg. I'm wearing a billowy, white, broderie anglaise tunic dress which gives him plenty of hiding space.

We get through the doors and approach the desk, and I notice two doctors standing together with their heads leaning in and looking at us. I immediately recognize one of them as the mum of one of Ollie's classmates, she's gorgeous and always busy and I haven't managed to chat to her yet and now I really wish I had. I smile brightly. And then I notice they sort of don't really smile back. They are both giving me a really specific look which I've never seen before; at the time I just thought they weren't being particularly friendly and were in professional mode, but I now know it was a look of, 'that person's life is about to be turned upside down and we are the people who are going to ease you into it.' It was a completely one-way look. There was no consideration for what they themselves looked like. It was oddly bare. A look full of weight. These moments must happen a few times in a doctor's career, where you know something massive about a patient before they do and you are faced with telling them. I remember once reading an article about how it felt to break awful news. I wonder if they remember the moments as sharply as their patients. I suspect they do.

Well the mum friend breaks away and smiles, we re-introduce ourselves as fellow school mums and then she really quickly takes Albie off to free me up to be with Josh. We are immediately taken through to the triage room where the other doctor meets us. The ER nurse starts all the basic obs with Joshie, chatting to him. The doctor introduces himself carefully and calmly as a paediatrician from the children's ward. He tells us that the blood test results have shown some extremely low numbers, and given reason to suspect that further investigation will be needed, but they are of concern. Something like that. He doesn't say much and I notice that he doesn't summarise, he doesn't give us any kind of diagnostic words I can hold onto like 'glandular fever' or 'infection'. And then the next few minutes will stay with me forever.

As I am someone who likes conversation to flow, preferably with plenty of smiles, and this conversation is a bit slow, and I want the other person to feel comfortable with me, I begin with a vague, "So, erm, do you have any idea what is going on with him?"

There is a humungous pause while he stares at me. I notice that he has very smooth skin. He is what I call 'parent-age', by which I mean my own parents' age, and has dark hair and is very slight. He is wearing a friendly jumper over his shirt. He has small, kind, dark eyes.

He says very slowly and steadily, "The exact question you have asked me...has a very blunt answer." He pauses for ages after every few words. He continues, "I am someone who is prepared to be blunt in delivering that information. If you want me to."

I understand what is happening here: this man is buying me time. He is speaking really slowly with massive pauses and he is buying me time so I can brace myself that he is about to drop a f*cking bombshell.

"Yes. Ok," I say, staring straight at him. Josh is sitting quietly in the chair next to me watching the nurse typing stuff into a computer. A few more seconds pass. "So what do you think it is?" I hold my breath.

He tilts his head downwards so he is looking slightly up at my eyes, furrows his brow to make it clear he is not dicking around, and says the word so, so quietly that it is barely out loud, but moves his mouth very emphatically. "Leukaemia."

There is a small pause and then I say, "Right."

That was my reaction. I used to wonder what I would say if I was given some horrific news. Gasp? Burst into tears? Sink down onto the ground? Hyperventilate? In movies, women manage to well up elegantly, eyes brimming, without their noses sort of expanding and going bright red. Well now I know that I say a ridiculously British, self-contained, 'Right'. Like a tiny, terse, lemon pip. Not sure what this says about me as a person. The self-preservation hackles spring straight up.

Leukaemia. A thousand things whirl through my brain in a few tiny seconds. An image from those charity billboard ads you see in shopping malls of a skinny, sallow, sunken-eyed bald child with a naso-gastric tube smiling at the camera through their pain. The dazzling, sparkly-eyed smile of our beautiful adult friend A who lost her battle recently. A voice saying, "Nooo, there's a mistake, this will all be fine, you wait!" Not so much a denial, but a sort of blind faith that Joshie just isn't a sick child, he just isn't, he has had temperatures this past week but he doesn't fit the image you have of a child with cancer. Never has. He has round rosy cheeks, bright eyes, he is really strong, jeez he just stacked an entire ton of ironbark firewood for us single-handedly a few weeks ago. He is a lion.

I raise my eyebrows and look down. Then, looking sidelong at my beautiful boy swinging his legs on the chair next to me, I say very quietly to this nice, blunt paediatrician, "Soo...we lost a beautiful friend to that illness last year, and we have explained about good and bad blood cells to our sons, so Josh knows that word. We should be a bit careful about saying that loudly around him right now." Part of me flies up into the sky and looks down at me, boggle-eyed with astonishment that I am using a perfectly normal voice and also that I have already become 'we'. We the adults who know this fact, this horror, we have to protect him. But I don't want to be an adult who knows the horror. Anyway this is all pie in the sky because this horror won't turn out to be true. They will have screwed up at the pathology lab and mixed up his results with some other poor child who is more like an Actual Unwell Person. This doesn't happen to us. Not because we're smug or arrogant or anything, but because we've already had our drama with Scott's spinal cord injury (explanation imminent!), and besides all three boys are fit as fiddles.

Well ha bloody ha, scream the ancient Greek gods, just you wait, oh ye of blind faith. I read Classics as my degree. Latin and Ancient Greek have a firm hold on me.

CHAPTER 2

Still Day 2

The next couple of hours are a blur. I must have gone into survival function mode. The paediatrician gets me to call Scott, who had driven up to Sydney the previous night and has just arrived at work. He struggles to get his head around how it can really be so important that he needs to drive all the way back here. He needs to be here, this is big. I speak to him with immense dread; I hate exaggeration and Scott is partial to it, so I feel that even using the words 'they think it could be leukaemia' somehow puts me in a category of over-sensationalizing everything. It feels completely ridiculous. Plus I know this will send him spiraling into full panic mode; he does not handle health crises well. So to sidestep briefly out of Joshie's story into Scott's…

After a couple of decades of competitive rowing, downhill and telemark skiing, ocean racing sailing and razzing round the Nürburgring in a car with zero suspension, all lubricated with plenty of delicious booze, 'client entertainment', and sitting motionless at a desk when he was in the office, Scott's spine decided to go epically mental. It turned out he was predisposed to premature disc degeneration, which most of us get as we age, but for him this meant that at age thirty-eight one of the biggest, meatiest discs in his lower back prolapsed spectacularly, crushing the spinal cord and slowly but emphatically shutting down the nerves which control his entire lower body. Severe back pain (a familiar state for him) morphed over a matter of hours into a terrifying numbness beginning in his right foot and creeping up his leg... we joked with mirthless black humour about The Nothing in The Neverending Story, "The NOTHING is coming!" in shrill, squeaky voices. Well I did. Probably not really appropriate.

Anyway we were living in Abu Dhabi at the time; Ollie was two and Josh was four months old. Unbeknown to us this was a true medical emergency; you have to decompress the spinal cord immediately or the damage is permanent – wheelchair for life. But to us it was just slightly sinister that the pain had morphed from agony to a creeping numbness, so, feeling a little like we were overreacting, we called our friend Big Ollie, a doctor friend from university days who also happened to be living in Abu Dhabi at the time. Thanks to his quick thinking advice (that may be one of the most understated thanks I have ever made; we owe this spectacular man Scott's mobility, quite literally), we jumped in the car and barrelled down the Sheikh Zayed Road to Dubai. Here he was fast-tracked for an MRI, and once they saw the scan he was almost flung into the operating theatre by a team of grim-faced, terrifically highly-skilled South Korean neurosurgeons. In the time it took me to get the bugaboo pram out of the boot, click it together, put the brake on (I'm good), unstrap baby Josh from his car seat, strap him into the bugaboo, unstrap toddler Ollie from his car seat and lift him out, grab baby bag, lock car, and get up in the lift to the third floor, Scott was going under. A sweet nurse called Sunny gently told me that I should drive the babies home, do dinner-bath-bedtime as usual and she would call me when Scott came out of theatre, probably in around eight hours. Err, eight hours?

For me, this moment, standing outside an operating theatre in a foreign country, dammit an entirely foreign environment (we were not a family who had set foot in hospitals apart from to have babies) surrounded by busy multicultural medical professionals, toddler in one hand, buggy in the other, 6'3" husband being wheeled away from me flat out on a bed in that 'we are in a massive hurry but we are trained not to look like we are in a massive hurry' way... this was the moment that something in me shifted. My eyes welled up when he vanished through the swing doors, and it hit me: it's just me. These babies need caring for. Go down in the lift, smile at the babies, sing songs all the way home. Dinner-bath-bedtime. Wait for the phonecall from Sunny. This was my first moment of realization that if there isn't any option but to get on with it, then you just get on with it. Besides, driving on the Sheikh Zayed Road between Dubai and Abu Dhabi is kind of like playing a strange hybrid of Super Mario Kart and dodgems with supercars and the world's most powerful 4x4s, so the concentration required to get the three of us safely back home didn't leave any brain cells at all for emotion.

Sunny called late that night, about eight hours after I had left Scott as predicted, reassured me in her humble Korean way that they had done a good job, and told me I should come back in the morning as he would be in recovery and sedated all night.

The immediate days after that were surreal. He couldn't feel much below the waist, but his mostly-numb leg muscles just about remembered how to walk. Well, shuffle, with a zimmerframe, a few feet at a time. I heard myself 'jollying', not a word I had ever applied to my own behavior before. We have photos of baby Josh lying on Daddy's hospital bed playing with his stretchy physio terrabands. Ollie batted his eyelashes at all the nurses and toddled around splashing the water features (yes, hospitals in the UAE have water features), while Sayeed, an amazing male nurse from Somalia with a funky haircut, taught Daddy how to self-catheterise. It was Christmas and the ward staff Christmas party was on the balcony outside Scott's room and they played Gangnam Style again and again and again. My mum immediately flew out earlier than planned from the UK and helped us cope. Looking back I'm not sure quite how it all worked.

All this resulted in something called Cauda Equina Syndrome. The cauda equina is a bunch of nerve roots in the lower spine where all the nerves which govern the sensory and motor functions of the legs and pelvic area are bunched up, before they fan out all around the lower body. Cauda equina means 'horse's tail' in Latin, which gives exactly the right visual explanation. Scott was left with serious and permanent nerve damage in his lower body; he can walk with a leg brace and his paralysis is classified as 'incomplete' which means he does have some mobility. His injury is invisible, you can't tell from looking at him unless you study his gait, or if he is wearing shorts and you notice that one leg is wasted.

Before it happened, if someone said 'lower body nerve damage' to me I would have thought one word: legs. But it turns out leg nerves are fairly resilient, and a lot of other stuff happens in the lower body and those nerves are not so resilient. It is amazing how things which would have made you wince quickly become normal. Words that you would have felt awkward using become part of daily family vocabulary.

"Mummy what are we doing today?"
"Well first we have to zap over to the spinal supermarket to get a couple of boxes of Daddy's catheters because he's about to run out and forgot to order more AGAIN (eyeroll, yawn), then we're meeting Tilly and Penny at the playpark…"

The 'new normal'. It was a massive lesson for both of us, me and Scott, that you just don't ever know what is going on behind the exterior that people choose to show you. We all know that, we read articles and blogs and people's experiences, but when you experience it first hand it hammers it home like nothing else can.

But what this left us with, and of course particularly Scott, was a deep-rooted panicky fear that any pain in his back meant that was going to happen again. And with one wasted leg (irreverently called the 'twiglet') supported by a carbon fibre leg brace, and seriously damaged pelvic nerves, if it happened again on the other side and took out his left leg he wouldn't be stable enough to walk. So at the first flare up he would descend into a frankly blind panic. Silent, white-faced, gruff with the boys, snappy with me at best, completely blank and mentally absent at worst. And I have a really low tolerance for moody husbands. I laugh, but it's not a good feeling when you have little ones running around and you know you're modelling a snippy snappy grumpy quick-to-anger marriage.

On a practical level, Scott would be mentally and to some extent physically paralysed by panic and fear, and my response, after getting really angry and frustrated at his mental paralysis (which would have zero effect) was to rush to organize a short-notice MRI scan for him 'to see what was going on in there'. We'd fork out the few hundred dollars each time only to see that yes, the discs were severely degenerated and yes at some point the discs above and below the gap where the other one had been would indeed give out. Physio would relieve the immediate pain, nothing would relieve the psychological fear and burden. The GP explained how the mind goes into a 'panic loop'; once in that state of panic it causes muscles to tense up which in turn exacerbates the physical pain, which makes you worry more, so you tense up more, and so it goes on. After a few days of physio, the pain would fade and Scott would revert back to his normal self, I would be high with relief and equilibrium would return, until the next flare up.

Scott's not unusual in having the back pain, some sobering statistic suggests that a huge proportion of the global adult population suffers from horrible back pain and then the associated psychological depression alongside it, but I think there's something particularly rough about being a man at that age and having the cauda equina stuff to deal with. Every medical professional he sees is openly fascinated and frankly aghast that it happened to him so young. And the other facet to it is the invisibility of his injury. His neuro consultant is slightly fixated on this; if you appear outwardly mobile and normal, no-one can tell there's anything wrong or different, so they don't make allowances. We had never considered the camber of a pavement before – now if he is walking in the CBD streets he has to calculate his path far in advance as he can't dodge pedestrians coming towards him or make those tiny physical shifts and manoeuvres we humans do without thinking. You can't chat with him while he's navigating as his male brain is fully occupied calculating where to put his feet next, in five paces, what to avoid. I tried persuading him that a sporty stick might make him look like a retired or injured Olympian, but he was having none of it. Over time, he learns to respond to the occasional judgmental comment as he comes out of a disabled bathroom with a level-headed, "Not all disabilities are visible."

We always said two things:
1.   Thank god it was one of us two, not one of the children.
2.   Thank god it was 'mechanical', not something creeping and insidious and evil like cancer.

Oh how the ancient Greek Furies must have been listening and LAUGHING in our faces!

One upside: we were already battle-hardened.

One downside: we were yet to learn that just because you've had one traumatic experience, it doesn't mean you won't get another.

So back to Josh and our local hospital. The paediatrician speaks to Scott on my phone, and tells him to drive calmly and safely (I have by this point told him about Scott's spinal stuff).

They have to get a cannula into the back of Josh's hand and get him on hefty broad spectrum antibiotics for whatever the infection is that he has been fighting. This was actually probably one of the worst moments we've had. It took three attempts, he was terrified, there were about eight faces all leaning over him on a big high hospital bed (a bed he now knows really well and plays around with, pressing the buttons to make it go up and down and giggling), each trying their own particular brand of 'calm down'... The doctor trying to do it has a shocker with two needles coming out of their sheath inside his vein or something, and instead of getting on with helping Josh cope with the terror she complains about her equipment. Fiiiiinally it is in, his whole hand and forearm strapped onto a 'surfboard', with an enormous red shiny brachiosaurus sticker stuck on it so he doesn't have to see it. He knows exactly who stuck the needles in him and still eyes her with deep suspicion.

Somehow I manage to get through to two friends who drop everything and come to the hospital to help with Albie. I don't remember how I contacted them, I just remember their angelic presence and wide, petrified eyes reflecting my wide, petrified eyes. They bring food, takeaway coffees and much needed support. It feels like nurses are kind of everywhere. We know them all now (this is still at our local hospital) and they are all gorgeous. They must have been completely sideswiped by this floppy-haired, rosy-cheeked, scared five year old whose life was about to go insane. Looking back, the feeling that they all must have known before we really believed it is really weird.

We are put in a room on our own (he basically has no immune system at all, although we don't know or understand this yet), and as soon as Scott arrives we manage to persuade Josh to let one of the friends sit with him so the paediatrician can talk to me and Scott on our own. We sit at a round plastic table in the hospital playroom, big plastic toys, dvds and books all around us. A particularly cheery plastic dinosaur grins manically at me. We are calm, the paediatrician is calm as he explains to us slowly that as well as having critically low blood counts, they also spotted some 'suspicious cells' in Joshie's blood. This phrase is used time and time again until we get the formal diagnosis. Suspicious cells. When we press him really hard to tell us if there could be another diagnosis he does a very good job of describing sepsis. But something about his words, his manner, his incredibly careful choice of vocabulary makes it blatantly clear to me that he thinks he knows what it is. Scott doesn't pick up on the certainty and sits on his fence.

The paediatrician says one thing which sticks in my mind for months to come, and serves me well whenever I have moments of 'what if he dies' over the coming weeks. He says that if it is confirmed that he has leukaemia, then although we as parents will be absolutely floored and devastated by this news, we need to keep in mind that an oncologist will get that diagnosis and immediately think, 'Right, let's solve this, let's get to work and sort it out.' I think he even rubbed his hands together as he said it, or I may have made that up. In other words, people will allow us our emotional turmoil because that is to be expected, and normal, but they will waste no time in getting started. Actually now I think about it that may have been a subtle hint at the speed at which things would start happening. The pace of the treatment and the onslaught of chemo doses is staggering. More on that later.

He explains to us that Josh will be transferred in an ambulance, which is on its way to us now, to one of the children's hospitals in Sydney. We have a choice; the paediatrician gently explains that both are excellent hospitals and he has no hesitation whatsoever in referring us to either, but this decision is likely to have a big impact on the next few months of our family life as we will probably be spending quite a bit of time there. We opt for the hospital slightly closer to Scott's parents. We also have a friend there who is a nurse who used to tell incredibly impressive and reassuring (and not confidential) stories, and another friend's father is a cardiologist there; these tenuous threads of familiarity add reassurance. The paediatrician tells me to make a list of things I will need for a week in hospital. 'WTF' again flashes in massive letters in front of my eyes. Did he just say a WEEK? Surely, like, the rest of today is disruption enough...maybe overnight would be a pretty horrible adventure... I'm breastfeeding

Albie, I've never been apart from him for longer than a hairdressing appointment. This is starting to slide out of control.

Ever obedient, I make my list. Josh is asking when we can go home. How the hell do I tell him what lies ahead, even just for the next two hours? You're going in an ambulance. You have always wondered what it would be like. And when we get to where we are going, there will be really bright strip lights and no windows and a hundred new faces all poking and prodding asking you questions and trying to get you to treat them like your friend, and calling you 'Buddy' and 'Little Man' and things which are not your name. I fudge it. I can't break this news yet. I haven't even computed it in my own brain.

Scott and I work out the next couple of hours. He drives home, packs my bag with the things on my list, picks up Albie from our wonderful friends, picks up Ollie from school, by which time Joshie and I are being loaded into a real live ambulance. Scott drives straight to his parents and I assume kind of falls into their arms and hands over the little boys.

Josh and I are strapped into our ambulance by Jane and Jenny, wonderful sturdy paramedics with ready smiles and loud voices. They are a breezy, energized change from the hushed concern of the ward. Josh is given colouring books, stickers, a cuddly bear, anything to keep him on side. Up to this point in my life, I had never been in an ambulance, this is a real one with very medical-looking equipment, not a patient transfer vehicle. We set off and I stare through the tinted windows at our local high street. Everything looks so bloody normal. Everyone is just doing normal stuff. How, what...? What just happened this morning? I want to scream, 'STOP!!!' at the planet, rewind, stop, stop we have taken a wrong turning, this is not how it is supposed to go today!! Instead I ask for the printout of the blood test results. I have no idea what I am expecting to do with this, it's not as if it will mean anything to me, but I wonder if it will say something concrete at the bottom that everyone may have inexplicably overlooked, like: Diagnosis: Actually Completely Fine. Jane readily hands it to me and I stare at it. Who am I kidding, this is a list of abbreviated scientific words which I wouldn't be able to interpret even if they weren't abbreviated, with numbers without any normal parameters next to them. Just random numbers rounded to two decimal points mostly. However even in my mental mist I can pick out that at least four of the numbers have next to them in capital letters: CRIT. Which I assume means 'critical'.

Joshie is strapped in a stretcher bed which magically went from on the ground at the loading bay to inside the ambulance without any apparent change in height. This is all totally new to us. It crosses my mind that he looks faintly ridiculous. Although subdued and clearly pissed off, he is a picture of health. Beautiful, radiant. He does not look like he has cancer. He starts colouring in some dinosaurs as best he can with his left hand strapped to a mini surfboard.

It is the middle of the night in the UK. I text my mum. I actually can't bear to look back over this text chain, but I recall sending her short one-liners, full of apologies for texting in the middle of the night but 'they think he has leukaemia'. No answer obviously as she is sound asleep. She was due to fly out to see us for Christmas in a few weeks' time, but I know that whatever is ahead, Scott and I cannot handle this and I tell her I need her to come out as soon as she can. I follow it up with, 'Wake up.' And then again, 'Wake up please.' The green whatsapp screen starts to swim as tears of panic finally win the battle. Josh cannot see me starting to cry, I grit my teeth and look resolutely out of the tinted windows.

I think it was about now that swearing really took on a whole new weight. For me, and I appreciate this will not be the case for everyone, I can't even begin to explain how satisfying it feels to swear about this situation. I look out of the window and think FUCK FUCK FUCK in my head. It's such a great sound to make, to articulate: it is short, sharp, the glottal 'u' sound preferably pronounced as royally as possible, the angry kicking 'k', and the aspirant and feisty 'f' at the start, it's perfect for expressing furious, outraged disbelief. It reminds me of a bit in the first Bridget Jones' Diary where Bridget describes how her irritating work colleague with big bum Perpetua is so posh that she says 'fack' instead of 'fuck'. That's taking it a bit far for me. The throatiness of the 'u' is perfect. I digress. Foul-mouthed linguistics, I love it.

The trees zoom by on the highway, traffic sounds muffled by the immense equipment inside the ambulance. At some point on the journey mum replies from the UK dawn saying she is already researching flights. She also offers a characteristic, 'Don't worry it will all turn out to be fine.' This is very much in the spirit of our family – when I was growing up we were ridiculously robust, mud-eating, germ-exposed, fully vaccinated 70s and 80s kids, I don't recall any GP appointments apart from for a routine hearing test and vaccinations. My brother broke his arm once falling out of a tree in our garden which was miserable for him and also very exotic, but apart from that we were a physically strong family, parents included, apart from the annual bouts of my dad's Man Flu which were treated with the daftest gravity – I still remember once on holiday in our campervan in Italy, my dad making the most monstrous fuss of sweating off a common cold under a duvet, and mum valiantly taking me and my little brother off to view yet another Roman site or something, and my brother berating me for being dismissive about Dad with the legendary words, "K!? Dad could DIE you know!" Oh how we laughed. So despite these very occasional attacks of highly patient-specific hyperchondria, I do not come from a family of drama or sickness. Extremely lucky to have good genes. So, mum's Pollyanna-style 'it'll all turn out to be fine' is predictable and understandable, but deep down I think I already know she is wrong. That paediatrician who eased me into this hellish day was a highly experienced man probably within a decade of retirement; he would not have used that L-word lightly. I want so badly to believe mum that this will all be a terrible scare and there will have been some mistake.

We get to the big children's hospital Emergency department and the day gets a bit less soft and cuddly. As Jane and Jenny our paramedics leave to go back to their ambulance I want to cling onto their arms and beg them not to leave us, I am in a foreign country here, you are our last remaining lifeline to our Normal Life, don't go, please don't go… Instead I thank them profusely, desperately, and encourage Josh to wave goodbye and thank them for driving so well. As they go I am smiling and waving but I am sobbing inside. Deep breath. Here we go.

The paediatrician back home had told me he was sending us to be admitted into the care of one of the oncologists who he had worked with previously (at this hospital in fact) and was extremely highly regarded. In my naivety at how hospitals work I thought this would mean that we'd arrive, sign a few bits of paper, maybe Josh would be triaged, and then we would see him. Nope. The busy ED is full (though not by UK NHS standards, everyone is still smiling and cheery because this is Australia, and 'full' just means that we are wheeled pretty quickly into a corridor and seen there rather than being wheeled to an actual ward bed). A doctor does our admission admin, I sign something agreeing that this will all be free (oh Australia you really do some things spectacularly well), and a nurse called Kate looks after us – one of those picture-book perfect nurses who is young, full of energy in her navy scrubs, with a friendly efficiency and a ready smile. I feel safe with her. She would be my friend if Josh didn't have suspected leukaemia and she wasn't working. Far out. More blood tests through the whacking great surfboard cannula on his hand. He HATES it. I hate it too. More stickers, more lollipops.

One thing that I am grateful for and really didn't dawn on me for days is that at no point did I need to explain anything to anyone or tell anyone anything. The system here works in a way that people really do take notes and pass them on to the right person who really does read them. I think the most I had to do for really the first few days was confirm Josh's personal details again and again and again, and apart from that I was a receiver of information, not a distributor. I never had to grope and grasp to find exhausted words to explain who he was and what was happening. This, when you are in massive shock and functioning on practical autopilot, is absolutely invaluable and I feel faint with gratitude about it really. I cannot begin to imagine how it must be for people who go through similar scenarios in countries where you don't get that.

We are put in a random room on our own in the Emergency department while they work out where to admit us. I don't realise at the time, but we are being isolated and kept away from other humans as much as possible as Josh basically has no immune system. At this point Scott and I are in contact from time to time on the phone and he reminds me that the paediatrician did mention sepsis; perhaps we won't be admitted into oncology. There is talk of us spending the night in the ER room as there is no bed available on the ward. It is still only mid-afternoon, they are talking about spending the night. This won't be sorted in the next eight hours then. I look around the room. It's an office. It has the bed that Josh was wheeled in on, a tv, and a plastic chair. Hmm. Then, suddenly, a bed becomes available on the ward after all. Hooray! A porter arrives and together with Kate we are wheeled off.

After wheeling along corridors and round corners and giving up on any sense of direction, we go through some heavy double doors and enter a lively, bright, pink and purple space with nurses at computers, and more nurses walking up and down a cheery corridor with doors off it. There are no curtains and no beds in rows like sausages, which, being British, is what I thought a ward would look like. A door of a room opens and slowly a clunky, cumbersome, tall metal pole on wheels emerges with a little computer beeping halfway up it, followed by a little person who has tubes hanging out of the bottom of their t shirt connecting to the little computer, followed by a mum, slightly hunched over the child, smiling brightly and talking softly. The child has no hair. F*ck. This is an oncology ward. They have brought us straight to the oncology ward.

Rising panic in my chest, almost rising vomit. Oh my god. I cannot do this. Where is Scott. Why is every nurse giving me a big welcoming smile? What the actual, what...?

They take us to the end room at the very end of the corridor, past every other room. I don't look in any of them. We walk into a room which seems to be full of really bright curtains. There is someone else in our room, in a bed, they have no hair. Something pink on the bed. It must be a girl. A machine beeps and makes ticking noises next to her and she doesn't move. My brain is going in slow motion and also fast forward. The mum is sitting next to the bed quietly, she is in full abaya and headscarf. (This beautiful family become smiley ward-friends, they are Indonesian and their sweet youngest daughter has a brain tumour.) The porter positions Joshie's bed and we draw the curtains around us. The curtains are printed with psychedelic Australian animals. Technicolour koalas, echidnas, and frill-necked lizards cocoon us. Oh my god.

So as life experiences go, zapping in a matter of hours from the school run to a paediatric oncology ward is confronting. Very confronting. I feel like an alien. I feel horror at the blatant, visible suffering of what I assume are incredibly, probably terminally ill children. Then I immediately feel shame – how can I feel horror, these are little humans, not something to be horrified by for goodness' sake, get a grip!? I feel shocked into an almost incandescent humility that this place has been existing here all this time while I've been going about my regular normal life, a parallel universe while the rest of the world orders lattes and gets stressed about whether they are getting enough Me Time. I feel weirdly removed and confident that this was all a mistake and soon I'll smile sympathetically at the parents of these poor beautiful children as we walk out, the human embodiment of relief, thanking our lucky stars that everyone was wrong and hoping we never set foot in such a terrifying place again. I feel dread, dread that everyone is not wrong.

They don't admit you onto a ward unless they are pretty sure. A small voice in my head keeps saying, "But don't they have to do a bone marrow biopsy to confirm leukaemia? He only said 'suspicious' cells, he didn't say they definitely saw leukaemia cells. He also mentioned sepsis. We don't know anything for sure until they've done the biopsy."

Scott arrives with Ollie and baby Albie. Ollie hugs Josh, asks him if he is feeling ok and admires his brachiosaurus surfboard arm. Scott looks at me, having just walked all the way down that corridor, and his knees start to buckle, his face crumples. I've never seen a man's face crumple before, this is awful, awful. He is 6'3", strong dark hair, dark beard, still wearing his smart work clothes from his morning in the office, he can't crumble, that doesn't compute for me. Shit he is about to lose it. He shoots a terrified look towards the other bed in the room and back to the door and says in a really wobbly voice, "Darling...I can't..." tears fill his eyes and he is gasping for air.

Something in me clicks, this is the same as before in that blasted hospital in Dubai five years ago; I have to find a way to get him upright and get him capable again. All I want to do is collapse into his chest and sob but that is not going to work, he can't hold me up, I've got to hold him up. Metaphorically, psychologically. Jesus maybe even physically. A distant part of my stomach thuds with disappointment; how I would love to be able to be the weaker one now. Be the willowy, red-eyed wife with strong hairy arms holding her up. But I can't, that's not us. One of us has to hold it together and forge on through, and that is going to have to be me.

I grab his upper arms hard through his linen jacket and get right in his face. At 6' tall I can almost level with him. Quietly, forcefully I say, "I know. I know. I know. Breathe. You can do this. Take a deep breath." It's like we do with the boys when they get angry, take a deep breath come on do it with me ready count to three ok ready one, two, three and deeeeep breeaaath…. Shoulders down ok better let's try that again ready one, two, three…

29

A long, steady, unbroken monologue so they don't have time for their own thoughts, all they can do is hear the instructions, hear the calm-down. Follow the instructions Scott, breathe, function, find your inner practical robot.

He doesn't find his inner practical robot, actually that may be a weird-but-helpful character flaw that is unique to me, but he calms down enough to help me come up with a logistical plan for the next twenty-four hours. At this point Albie is breastfed when he wakes up in the morning and then at bedtime, I feed him to sleep every night. At some point in the ambulance I had wondered if he would stay with me in the hospital, but now I'm here on this oncology ward there is absolutely no way that could happen. Scott can't stay on the ward because a) Josh's heart would break if I left him now, and b) Scott's still-recovering back needs a proper supportive bed – he will wake up lame and in pain if he attempts a night on a pull-out armchair. He is also someone who cannot function at all on a bad night's sleep. (Not for us the sharing of newborn nightfeeds; let one of us be crippled with tiredness so the other one at least has a relatively normally functioning brain.) We work out that Scott and the boys will stay with his parents, half an hour from the hospital. My mum will go straight there from the airport when she lands from the UK in about twelve hours. Scott will bring the boys to me each morning and evening so I can feed Albie.

I feed him. Part of me marvels at the female body; despite the shock and strain of the day, my boobs are still ready and relieved when he drains them. I look down at his fluffy little blond head, his eyelashes curved on his cheek, completely relaxed, knowing in this moment only the safety and security of mummy and breastmilk. Scott and his mum will have to put him to bed, the first time anyone has put him to bed apart from me. He's never had a bottle, we don't even have any, he's never had any formula or cow's milk. I could never be bothered to express as it seemed like yet another thing to do; breastfeeding just seemed the lazy option and I am inherently lazy. How the hell is this going to work? I wish someone could have popped their head down out of the sky and whispered in my ear, "Hey listen – you're about to learn the hard way that that baby is the happiest-natured, most chilled-out little dude you could ever have wished for, and he and your other son are about to get enfolded in a tidal wave of love from their grandparents, you have nothing at all to worry about." But of course no-one poked their head down from the sky, and I had to make a conscious decision Not To Worry About That. Compartmentalisation is about to become my default setting. Open the drawer, put it in, and close the drawer until the right time comes to open it and deal with it.

Scott is completely knackered. He has driven all the way from Sydney up to the Highlands, been whacked round the head with horrific news, gathered up his boys, driven back up here and now has to drive half an hour to his parents' house. His back is hurting, his semi-paralysed leg is limping despite his leg brace and he is close to breaking point, not that I know what that would constitute exactly. I wonder if we should get his dad to come over in a taxi to drive them all back in our car. Scott insists he can handle it and goes to get the car leaving the three boys with me. We all cuddle and hug Joshie and tell him how brave he is. I have literally no idea how I stay dry-eyed through this. All I can attribute it to is the fundamental parental need not to stress out the boys; my tears might introduce the idea that things were out of control, and the older two in particular really need to feel safe and contained. Maybe it's that, maybe I am still so shocked I have no tears.

Scott is gone forever. I ring him again and again, how far away did you park?! Finally he answers and he is hysterical; he has driven the car into a bollard in the car park and broken the wing mirror. This is a man who adores cars, spends five hours 'valeting' them (putting black stuff on the tyres, polishing the inside of the window buttons, I mean seriously). On a good day, smashing up a wing mirror would wreck his day. I need to keep this really simple. "Drive to the pick up zone and we will meet you there now. Take a deep breath."

I explain to Josh that I have to walk Albie and Ollie to the car and will be five minutes. The nurse stays with him, he is teary and silent. It strikes me that every single thing today is just so awful. It's dark outside now, I load the little ones into their seats and go round to the driver's window. Scott has tears falling down his cheeks into his beard. His hands are shaking. He really does not look safe to drive. Far out, this is insane. I try once more to suggest his dad comes but he is adamant he can handle it. He is incredibly safe, infuriatingly so on a normal day, such a nerd about the rules of the road, I trust him completely even now. However he needs to hear the right thing. I think fast.

"Darling you have one job to do right now. Do not think about anything. You have one job, and that is to get Ollie and Albie safely back to your parents. Drive safely. That is it. If they cry, just drive safely. Just. One. Job."

He nods and sort of visibly pulls himself together. This works on him; clear, direct, unambiguous words. I wave them off, and turn back towards Josh.

When I get back I have to create bedtime. I noticed a little library in the ward playroom as I walked back into the ward, and Josh agrees to have a bedtime story. I find my favourite of all our boys' books: Tiddler by Julia Donaldson. I make Josh as comfy as I can around his stupid surfboard, recline his bed, puff up his pillows and pull up his blankets, try everything I can to make this sterile place feel snug. I start reading, I know it so well I don't need to look at the pages: "Once there was a fish and his name was Tiddler, he wasn't much to look at with his..." oh my god I can't read my voice is cracking. I have picked my favourite book which WE SHOULD BE READING AT HOME IN HIS BUNK BEDS! This is all wrong, this is all so, so awful. My heart feels like it is breaking, it hurts under my sternum. This is the hardest thing I have had to do today, harder than watching all the needles, harder than staring at the smooth-faced paediatrician, I've GOT to read him Tiddler without crying. Why the hell did I choose my favourite book, I must be out of my mind?! I grit my teeth, take a steadying breath and somehow, god knows how, read on. My throat is agony, throbbing, forcing out words. He responds a bit, enough for me to know my boy is still in there, his spirit isn't totally crushed.

Finally, after the story, I crumble. All day long he has been begging me to go home. When can we go home, can we go home after this doctor has finished talking? Can we go home now mummy? I just really want to go home, please mummy? With the corners of his mouth turned down and big shiny tears in his brown eyes, please please can we go home now. It is so hard to come up with the right answers; I agree with him, I desperately, desperately want so badly to go home. I want to be at home watching another episode of The Good Wife with Scott lying on the sofa, while the boys snore and fart and sleeptalk in their rooms, rolling my eyes if one of them wakes and interrupts the trials of Lockhart-Gardner... God how I want that, it is breaking me! I lean my head into his sweet soft neck and screw my eyes tight shut and whisper, "I know, I know, I want to go home too, this is SHIT, it is SHIT Joshie and I am so, so sorry this is happening." He is wide-eyed and I can feel his awestruck silence, Mummy said a really bad word. It's just the best word for what is happening. The only word. (And oh my he is going to hear me saying some bigger words than that in the next few months.) I continue, "But we are a team Joshie, you and me, and I am going to be next to you and with you all the time. I am not leaving you on your own anywhere here, and you are going to be safe. Everyone here wants to help make you better. We are a team and I love you." He falls asleep, corners of his beautiful rosebud mouth still turned down. I feel oddly lonely now he is asleep.

Much later that night, when I am trying to curl up on a narrow pullout armchair bed and Joshie is breathing deeply and sound asleep, exhausted and defeated after the day of needles and ambulance and hell, a Registrar comes in. I think he was called Lawrence or Nick or Rob or something. He is in full operating theatre clothes, he might even be English, and I can tell he is about my age and we probably went to university together or he probably knows my mates who became doctors. I think they are probably Registrars now. Maybe consultants. All this goes through my head while he introduces himself and then says, somewhat haltingly, "So I'm not sure how much you've been told…"

He is clearly at the end of an exhausting day of work, but has taken the time to swing by this new admission on the oncology ward before he heads home to, let's say, sushi tonight with his fiancé. I feel like I know him, he is such a familiar type - I bet he has a wicked sense of humour and has on occasion hooked himself up to a saline drip after a massive night out once or twice to avoid a hangover - but to him I am just an exhausted hospital mum who's just taken her contact lenses out and is still adjusting to her glasses. Actually he definitely doesn't think that, he probably just sees 'parent in a camp bed'. I assume he is asking me a question so I answer.

"Err. They think he might have leukaemia so are doing a bone marrow aspirate in the morning, so he can't have anything to eat in the morning because it is a general anesthetic." (Despite the insanity of what I just said, I feel briefly proud that I clearly listened to instructions, and I used the word 'aspirate'. My inner Hermione Granger smiles smugly.)

"Yes. Has anyone spoken to you about a central line?"

"Yes, they said that might happen if it does turn out to be leukaemia..." I trail off, clearly my unspoken words being, 'which it OBVIOUSLY ISN'T because that would be COMPLETELY RIDICULOUS and NOT VERY 'US' and ABSOLUTELY NOT OK.'

"Ok, so we are confident enough in the diagnosis that we think it is best to put the central line in during the same general anaesthetic when he has his bone marrow aspirate and lumbar puncture, so he doesn't have to go through two general anaesthetics in a short space of time. So that can be done tomorrow at the same time provided you understand and are comfortable with that."

Oh my god. Joshie has leukaemia.

CHAPTER 3

Still Day 2

I have no idea what I said to Lawrence-Nick-Rob. Ever polite, I probably mumbled some form of thanks. Yeah thanks for basically confirming the last twelve hours' fears just as I crawl into 'bed' and am completely alone apart from my sleeping son, lying a couple of metres away from strangers. It's not his fault, from his point of view he needed to establish what I had been told and presumably didn't want me to have a horrible shock and potentially cause a massive fuss tomorrow and get in the way (they don't know me yet, massive fusses are not something I do when people are stopping my child from, err, dying. Fainting with gratitude is more my style).

I roll onto my side, my face an inch from the blue fake-leather side of the armchair. My stomach is caving in. I make a fist and jam my knuckles into my mouth and screw my eyes tight shut and cry absolutely terrified, silent tears. The mum sharing our room lying on her identical armchair bed next to the girl with the brain tumour must be able to hear me gasping for air, stifling it like mad. I also know, already, that she has been here too and knows not to offer any comfort yet. I consider going out into the corridor and finding a nurse to have a breakdown on. Then I realize I am so exhausted I am probably better off lying down.

Thoughts whirl.
Every parent's nightmare.
This fresh hell.
This hellish Now.
I feel like my heart is breaking. Actually slow-motion breaking, cracking apart, I can feel it.
Scream into the wind. That bloody 'Scream' poster everyone had at university.
I want to climb to the top of a freezing mountain being blasted by a Himalayan icy wind and scream into the spindrift, scream spindrift out of my mouth like a dragon breathing fire.

The profound shock at this is... I struggle to find the words. Josh hasn't been unwell. It isn't like we had some nagging, underlying suspicion that something wasn't right, something needed fixing. Apart from these very recent few days of fevers he is a really strong child. Of our three boys, Ollie has always been super-skinny and had itchy skin after swimming lessons, Albie is a delicious chunky baby who was born with a little bright red storkbite on his forehead, gets a bit cross about growing teeth and has had the odd cold but is pretty stoic, and Joshie in the middle had a bit of viral induced wheeze as a baby ('viral induced wheeze' is the artist formerly known as 'asthma', but apparently because they often grow out of it they are reluctant to give an asthma diagnosis these days, and as predicted he hasn't had issues with it for three years) but he is tough, really tough, and physically strong. He is our little brown nut with stripy gold hair, sturdy olive limbs, boundless stamina and energy. And by nature he is steadfast, thoughtful, kind, stubborn. Can easily hold his own with his older brother Ollie, and is also very happy playing on his own for ages; he loves his own company but is self-assured, not a loner. Where Ollie is an airy sprite, Josh is an earthy stomper. Grounded. Logical, pragmatic, inquisitive. He doesn't get particularly anxious, and if something worries him he comes to me or Scott and gets it straight in his head so the worry evaporates. I think he is a genuinely resilient child – and I want to be really clear that I'm not saying any of this in a self-congratulatory, proud, 'aren't we great parents' kind of way, more in utter, paralyzing bewilderment that this little person could actually have leukaemia. Leukaemia for god's sake!? I just read a book where the fictional main character is thinking about terrible childhood illnesses and she says, 'meningitis, leukaemia…' I mean it's right up there, every parent's nightmare. Your child getting cancer.

Obviously we ponder on this a lot in the weeks to come; what did we miss? Were there any signs? Could we have known? I do remember watching his little body climbing into the bath in the middle of Winter, and thinking the skin on his body looked pale and he looked a little bonier than usual, but I just thought it was mid-Winter, he was having a vertical growth spurt and made a note that we must hotfoot it to the beach for some Vitamin D and sea salt the minute it warmed up a fraction. I also had a strange, mild sense of guilt that I wasn't spending enough really good quality time with him; I should be reading more books to him, cuddling him more, he occasionally had a slightly sad expression and was quicker to cry than he used to be. I put this down to his age, him being the middle child, me having a baby and being exhausted from broken nights. I think I baked a cake with whipped cream and berries the day I identified this guilt and thought I was cheering us all up by having a proper family afternoon tea. (Ha! Fixing the problem with a cream cake – bit of a contrast to months and months of aggressive chemo.)

Scott says now that he sometimes watched Josh playing on the pirate ship in our garden in the weeks before his diagnosis, and thought he seemed a bit less adventurous than usual, more cautious, sometimes stopping to take deep breaths. But we didn't even mention it to each other, none of these observations was anywhere near serious enough to cause concern, it was all just normal family stuff as far as we knew. And besides we were tough, strong, healthy, fortunate. Should we have connected the dots, were there even dots to connect? Knowing now what some of the signs of leukaemia are, I think his body was doing a pretty good job of seeming normal.

I'm forty as I write this. By now I have watched and am watching several friends in my generation fight different types and stages of cancer, seen older dear friends fighting hard, lost the beautiful previously-mentioned friend A to leukaemia, and then of course if you go one step further removed, cancer is everywhere – friends' mums, sisters, fathers, uncles, neighbours, famous people... I am relatively well-versed in the language of adult cancer. But I don't know any children with cancer. I know of one friend's niece who also had leukaemia. Paediatric oncology. What a horrible, cruel word-pairing.

When we start to tell people about his diagnosis they are shocked; his preschool teacher says in genuine amazement that he is the last child they would have picked as having leukaemia. Dear friends at home who we see regularly are absolutely floored: but he isn't sick, he doesn't look ill, this could be any one of us.

Starting the following morning, the level of support we receive from 'the System', which deserves a capital S, is nothing short of extraordinary. From the moment of diagnosis it is like a well-oiled machine clicking into action. We are barely on our own for more than a few minutes. We are now firmly embedded in our room behind our psychedelic curtains. We are shown the ward's Parents' Room: hot water, toaster, microwave, freezers packed full of big bags of food with name labels on them – note to self: this is clearly a ward where people stay for a long time – posters offering support everywhere, a huge range of really gorgeous teas and coffees, help-yourself ice creams and treat foods, magazines, a massive library of dvds, squishy sofas... All the nice stuff has stickers on it saying 'Redkite'. I have a very vague memory of seeing that logo before in the supermarket, a charity thing maybe. Little do I know Redkite is going to become one of the main supports to get us through this.

I notice that there are tiny, unobtrusive cctv cameras all over the place. I later find out from one of the other mums that this is so the nursing staff can see if a parent goes in there and breaks down; support is only ever moments away. This staggering example of the wholistic kindness, the all-encompassing humanity of the people who run this strange parallel universe makes me want to cry. We know, we know what you are enduring. You are not alone. You are NOT alone. The Nursing Unit Manager later tells me, "You have one hundred and fifty new friends now." And she only means the nursing staff, that doesn't include the other parents, the doctors, the admin and support people... All supporting you as you join a club that no-one wants to join.

The deluge of medical information begins. We have a team of people assigned to looking after Josh, and, as is repeated to us over and over again, looking after us as a family. A pyramid with an oncology god at the top (the one Josh was referred to by the paediatrician at the hospital back home), followed by his colleagues, the team nurse, the outreach nurse, the ward nurses (this is probably not in the right order for the pyramid, but gives an idea of the scale of the support and care), the child life therapists, the social workers, a chaplain even comes round (oh my god please this is too much, chaplains come round to do last rites don't they? Please go away! Oh actually it's just to say that 'we are with you for every step of your journey if you would like us to walk with you, regardless of your faith', which is undeniably the very essence of goodness). And the heavenly Redkite lady. She is Belgian and speaks with a strong Belgian-French accent. She appears in a quiet moment and doesn't try to say too much or empathise, we chat more in the days that follow, but to my amazement she hands me an enormous holdall bag, red and white stripy, absolutely stuffed full of 'nice stuff'. Fleecy blankets, full size toiletries, water bottles, a keepcup, pens, notebooks, a 'cancer diary', vouchers for the hospital cafes, vouchers for fuel, vouchers for groceries, nice teabags, chocolate, all packed up with accompanying literature and booklets which all seem to say the same thing in various different calm-font headlines: We are with you every step of the way. We will help you navigate this new world. You are not alone. Do not feel alone. It is, in the truest sense of the word, awesome. My jaw drops. Josh helps me unpack it all and we murmur in amazement at each thing and arrange it all on our little table. We are drenched in wonder and gratitude, gratitude so intense it makes our brains fuzzy. We organize our Redkite stuff together; we organize our minds.

CHAPTER 4

Day 3

As we speak to these many, many medical professionals who will become the anchor points in our new normal, one things keeps being hammered home: a huge emphasis is put on the fact that paediatric cancer is completely different to adult cancer. The outcomes, the goals, the intensity of the treatment schedule… Everything happens lightning fast with children. There is hardly any waiting around for answers or waiting around to decide what to do next. Blood test results take forty minutes. Individualised treatment protocols are all set up and ready to go the minute you get your diagnosis. We find out the exact name of what Josh has: Pre-B Cell Acute Lymphoblastic Leukaemia. They tell us this is the 'best' type of leukaemia to have, with a 90-95% success rate. We stop and think what does that actually mean, what is a 'success'? It turns out that a success means they get rid of it completely and it doesn't come back for five years, by which time the child is considered cured. They say emphatically that the aim with this sort of leukaemia is to cure it for good; whereas the aim with many adult cancers is to manage them and prevent them from coming back too soon. They tell us to make sure we tell any friends and family who want to google it to type in 'paediatric ALL' not just 'ALL' because what you read is very different. They suggest that googling isn't a particularly wise idea anyway as every single child is different, and so is their treatment. We start to feel lucky. No professional, no one, suggests that we are lucky though, that conclusion and response is very much left up to us.

The following day Josh and I wake in the hospital and gather our thoughts. He is very quiet, big brown eyes full of fear. He is nil by mouth, so he can't even have a rallying breakfast. And because he is nil by mouth they don't bring any food at all, so I can't steal any of his food. I try to distract him with CBeebies on his tv and the exciting remote buttons. We don't have terrestrial tv at home, only streaming, so this is a whole new world of entertainment for him. Still it takes about ten minutes of promises and almost-bribes to get him to agree to me leaving him to go to the loo (the ensuites have signs that say they are strictly for patients only, and the parents' bathrooms are outside in the corridor). I sneak my keepcup and toothbrush out with me and practically run around the bathroom and parents' room. Still when I get back he is full of reproach and I feel awful. This continues for the entire first week, any time I need a wee or step further than a metre away from him he gets really scared. Time and time again I promise him that no-one here will hurt him or do anything bad to him, and that he can press his little 'nurse button' if he is worried about anything while I'm doing my speed-wee.

It is a busy day in the hospital, cases like Josh's which are short-notice admissions who need a non-emergency general anaesthetic, go onto what is called the 'emergency list', meaning that he is on the list to have his GA (general anaesthetic) at some point today, but he obviously gets trumped by for example a car crash victim, or someone whose case is more urgent. This is totally understandable common sense. While we wait our turn, our oncology god comes to see us with his entourage of concerned, awesome people. He explains the concept of the central line to me and Scott again. (Scott has joined us with the other boys and also his mum, so we have three adults and three little boys now. This frees me up to go for a wee and fill my coffee cup and put milk in it without running.)

At this point I have to say that although I have had friends in the UK with what was called a Hickman line, and I have vaguely heard about ports in the chest, I had never really considered the idea of exactly how and where it works. It actually makes me feel a bit queasy. It basically seems to constitute a part of the outside world going straight into your body, the inside world, with nothing to sort of bridge the two worlds. This is really odd for a non-medical brain to grasp. Well, it was for me. I listen, intently, as the oncology god describes how brilliant it is for children who are going to need around 7 months of intensive, very frequent chemotherapy doses and general anaesthetics, as they won't ever have to have a needle stuck in them, not once. After the three attempts experience on the first day I can totally see the appeal of this. He says many nurses think it is probably the most revolutionary thing in paediatric oncology of the past few years. I later chat to the chemo nurses and they concur (I love that word – I always picture Leonardo di Caprio in Catch Me If You Can nodding with a frown, "I concur, Doctor."), adding that the other massive breakthrough was the anti-emetic drug ondansetron, delivered in wafers which dissolve instantly on your tongue. Before they discovered that, and before they started using central lines, the nurses would be faced with a big room lined with armchairs with a little child in each one crying pitifully about the needle stuck in their arm and vomiting every few minutes into bags which had to be disposed of in a cytotoxic bin. It sounds like something out of Dante's Inferno.

Back to our central line. Despite my and Scott's attentive nodding and interested expressions, the oncology god is clearly also a psychic and can tell we have absolutely no idea how to envisage what he is talking about. He calmly suggests he find another family on the ward whose child has the same thing as Josh, who are further down the treatment path, who might show us their child's central line. We do this, and they are amazing. Little G is a bit younger than Josh and has another few weeks to go before she can have her line removed. She has no hair and is moody. Her parents are lovely. Her dad is a big, calm bear of a man who holds her right up near his shoulder. Her mum has a massive happy smile and a concerned brow and is full of energy. Later we talk more and she gives me invaluable tips and bizarre cancer-mum-hacks. I love her. She tells me I am doing brilliantly and that at this point she was in a heap on the floor in the parents' room. I tell her I am actually in a heap on the floor, this is just a weird out-of-body version of me. The oncology god nods, pleased.

As I walk back down the pink and purple oncology ward to our room, I grimace inwardly at the cruel twist of fate playing out in my new vocabulary; rewind ten years to my pre-Scott London life, and the Central Line was the line on the London Underground, red on the iconic map, which I would often use to get to and from dinners, work, dates, drinks… connecting old friends and new friends, bars and birthdays, keeping the human connections alive. Scott and I lived in London at the same time but never met there, but his nearest tube station was Shepherds Bush (conforming most pleasingly to the Aussie-in-London stereotype) on, of course, the Central Line. And now here we are, the central line keeping not so much the human connections alive, but our son alive. The impossible weight of it is so inconceivable it actually makes me gasp-laugh.

So Josh will have what is called a 'tunnelled double lumen central venous access line (CVL)'. It is a white, silicone-textured thin tube which comes literally straight out of his chest, à la Alien, somewhere to the right of his heart. Outside his body, it then divides into two white tubes, each with a white plastic clamp on them and then a bit further down either a red cap or a white cap. They dangle. Inside his body, the tube goes up under his skin to the base of his neck, where it then goes into the jugular vein (artery? I am not a medic, I am a Classicist and a word-nerd and a mum), and then, once it is inside the vein it doubles back down and goes straight into the vena cava (not actually a type of Venetian sparkling wine, but one of the veins which delivers blood straight into the heart). As there are two 'lumens' (dangly bits), it works both ways. They can put stuff into Josh through one, or both, and they can take blood through either too, although I think they usually use the red one. They can also do the two different directions at the same time, and they can also add more 'caps' once he is connected to lines (tubes) further down those lines, so that they can, for example, give him a general anaesthetic while he is on fluids and chemotherapy at the same time.

At the point where the line comes out of his chest, it is made into a wiggly shape, either an 'S' or a swirl, flat on his skin, before it is all covered with a sticky transparent dressing. The wiggle means that if anyone or anything were to pull on the dangly lumens (images of an Alsatian leaping up and grabbing them joyfully in his mouth make me feel sick with fear, not that we know any Alsatians) then it would first of all pull on the wiggle, not the actual entrance site.

They also make a tiny incision at the base of the neck at the point where the tube goes into the jugular, I assume as this must be the really fiddly bit for the amazing surgeon so they need access right at that point.

Back to our ward room. Nil by mouth ticks away, lunchtime approaches. As with the previous day, we are constantly visited by people giving us information and talking us through what is happening. We also have Albie, Ollie and Granny (Scott's mum) with us. It is a complete, total blur. One of the people is a Child Life Therapist. The job of these wonderful, amazing humans is basically, as far as I can understand, to make life for children in hospital more tolerable, more enjoyable and more emotionally functional. She is immediately christened 'the Lego lady', and with good reason. She brings boxes of Lego kits – not just a box of Lego, but actual kits with the instructions – and, like many boys his age, Josh is a Lego ninja. She clocks his slightly bored, disparaging response to the kit for age 5 – 8, and returns with the 8 – 14 stuff. Now we are cooking on gas. Nil by mouth is forgotten, he is totally absorbed. We have found our thing. Hallelujah. For the first time I feel my stratospherically high anxiety level sink down just a notch.

I can only speak for my own experience of course, but so, so much maternal energy is needed to keep yourself functioning on a practical level while also having, obviously, your child's immediate mental wellbeing at the forefront of your mind. And that's before you allow yourself to consider the bigger picture of your child's actual wellbeing, which is, in this case, so surreal and terrifying that it almost doesn't bear thinking about. Every second of every minute of every hour I am turned physically towards Josh, holding him, holding his hand, stroking his hair (his hair! Oh god! I cannot even think about this yet), listening to him, listening out for any brewing panic…It never eases. People ask how on earth you sleep in a pull-out armchair bed next to your child on a raised, sterile white hospital bed beeping away. Well I would sleep for a couple of hours at a time between nurse visits and I would sleep like the dead. I have never been so knackered.

A note on sleep: I have always considered myself terrifically lucky that at times of great stress – heart broken by my first boyfriend at university, or watching my spectacularly adulterous and self-righteous father and my naïve, ever-kind mother divorce, or Scott's spinal cord injury – I have been so exhausted by coping with the emotions of the day that my head hits the pillow and I pass out. I have very rarely found myself lying awake at night, thoughts swirling. I am unimaginably grateful that, so far, this character trait seems to be staying with me.

The Child Life Therapist also brings play dough, art and craft activities, and a big table with edges so the Lego doesn't fall all over the bed. She also gives both Josh and Ollie the most fantastic thing which I think demonstrates really well the attention that is given to families and siblings when a child is diagnosed. It is a laminated sheet of A4 with a big printout of a Lego man on it, but he has no head. Across the top of the page it says, 'TODAY I FEEL…' and then in a separate ziplock bag are about fifteen laminated cards with printed yellow Lego heads on them, each with a different expression. Above the head it says the emotion: 'ANGRY', 'EXCITED', 'HAPPY' etc. One face is blank, with no facial features and no accompanying word, so you can fill in your own word. You stick the body on the wall, and each day, or more than once a day, your child identifies what they are feeling, finds the appropriate head and sticks it on the body with blutak. I love this. As a mum of three boys I am hoping to bring them up so they know what they are feeling and can express their feelings, and crucially so that they can use their feelings to understand and empathise with other human beings. As digital and social media natives (unlike us immigrants, to borrow Ollie's former school principal's terminology) they will be fluent in the language of computers and digital communication, and so the humans who actually know how to interact with other humans, face to face, in person, will stand a better chance of reaching contentment, I reckon. So, back to the Lego men. They leap onto the little heads and begin a lengthy conversation about exactly what they feel like. Ollie concludes with 'EXCITED' and Josh uses the blank one to write 'HUNGRY'. I am not entirely sure that 'excited' demonstrates that he is grasping the gravity of what is happening with Josh, but this is a good start – 'sad' or 'worried' or 'anxious' would have broken my heart a little bit more than it is already breaking for Josh. And as for 'hungry', well there will come a time where we explain that hungry is not, technically, an emotion, but I make a note to myself that clearly nil by mouth trumps any feelings. Scott and I laugh despite all the awful stuff, the nurses think 'HUNGRY' is hilarious and stick it on his door – a message to all passing staff.

By late-afternoon it is clear that the emergency list was long and Josh has been bumped to the following day. They bring him a massive dinner. Another twenty-four hours of high anxiety to worry about central lines and bone marrow aspirates and things we didn't even know existed twenty-four hours previously. Although disappointing, this is also kind of a relief: as well as giving us more time to feel anxious it also gives me more time to make the mental adjustment to what is happening. Several senior medical staff come by to apologise and explain the reasons for the delay. I am astonished that they apologise; we are, through all the shock, profoundly grateful for every person, every second of attention, every iota of scientific knowledge, the gratitude we are feeling is almost a physical, palpable thing. It is like a cloak. A Gratitude Cloak. Josh was, unbeknown to us, dying before our eyes two days ago. That fact is SERIOUSLY frightening. These people, every single one of them, are working together to fix him. However much we wish this wasn't happening, it is, and we are unbelievably lucky to live in a time where people dedicate their entire lives to fixing these things.

When Josh is blissfully stuffing his little face with pasta and yogurt and jelly and ice cream and bread rolls and hot chips and carrots (it turns out that a child with leukaemia can still have a raging appetite, bit of a surprise), it dawns on me that perhaps not all parents feel grateful. Perhaps they were apologetic because people complain. This is such a weird concept to me. And fast-forward a few treatment sessions and I realize that some people love complaining. Maybe it's one of the ways that some of us humans cope with the immense stress and fear of what they're going through. I am probably irritating in the other extreme, profusely thanking every single person we meet.

I feel guilty when I recognize nurses' faces and can't remember their names, so I start making secret notes on them.

Mel: pillar box red hair, mad, fantastic
Haylee: looks like she should have the lead role in Swan Lake, clean blonde ponytail
Clare: Irish, short blonde hair, can sort anything out
And so it goes on. And on. One hundred and fifty new friends, the Nursing Unit Manager tells us. I will never forget that.

I love them all, I want to hug every single nurse who walks in and says, "Hi Joshua!" to which he replies, "Josh!" and I say brightly, every single time, "Say hello first Josh and THEN you can tell them your real name!" You are saving my child's life. To me, you are real live angels. I can practically see your wings under your scrubs.

Over the coming months I have long conversations with the nurses, and one or two of them talk about how if you work in paediatric oncology, doing long twelve or thirteen hour shifts six days a week, you begin to think of children with cancer as normal. Which they're not; it's incredibly rare, thankfully. One nurse describes seeing her nieces and nephews on her day off and catching herself thinking how amazing it was that they had hair, and how she panics every time they bump themselves or climb on something risky. She tells me that some of the nurses who have their own children quit when they realize this is happening and go into other areas of nursing in order to protect their own mental wellbeing and redress the balance of 'normal'. These nurses are amazing people, and as well as gratitude I have profound respect for how hard they work and much they care. Often they are red-eyed by the time they do the handover at the end of their shift. They all wear comfy shoes. They don't just do their job, they really care so much. The word 'nurse' doesn't feel enough, it's such a broad, humble, junior-sounding word. There is nothing, nothing junior about these people. Again I get that guilty feeling that this was all happening alongside the rest of the normal world and I had never considered what it was actually like.

Before we go to bed on that second night our nurse-friend who works on a different ward calls by to see us. I haven't seen her for a few months since we moved away from Sydney. She arrives laden with gorgeous helpful things; she knows the score. Blueberries, bananas, water bottle, a journal, chocolate, raisin bread, a whole box of kindness. The invisible 'emotion-me' bursts into tears but the robot-me holds it in for Joshie. I am becoming steely. She engulfs me in a big hug and I smell her clean, normal hair, she smells of normal life outside the hospital. I whisper a panicky F*CK...F*CK... into her neck. There are no other words, I can't find anything more eloquent, I know she won't be offended, and hidden and muffled from Josh I need another human to hear me express the inexpressible, the expletive.

Another night. Beeping, nurse buttons, squeaky armchair bed.

CHAPTER 5

Day 4

Another morning with no breakfast. Another CBeebies-while-I-run-for-a-wee (make that the fastest, sneakiest shower in the world actually). This time they are right onto us. We get a call from Scott to say he is on his way (with the boys and BOTH Grannies, my mum has arrived from the UK, my knees almost buckle with relief at this news! It's like your own mum's presence gives you permission to be weak, briefly anyway) and as soon as we hang up, the porter arrives along with an anaesthetist and we are off out of the ward and through the hospital, into a lift, up to the operating theatre. Joshie hates the loss of control and would rather walk, he hates being wheeled on his bed (this will become a theme as time goes by and he becomes known as the boy who insists on walking to and from his lumbar punctures). Someone finds him an ipad (it turns out they have hospital ipads for such moments, how amazing is that?) and shows him some weird gold-collecting running animal game and he willingly hides away in the game. I am so grateful at this point to Steve Jobs. In fact if Steve Jobs could pop back from the dead briefly to see the paediatric oncology ward and clinic waiting room, and the chemo room for outpatients, and see the delicious and total distraction that his devices provide for children who really, seriously need to be distracted - and their parents frankly who also need the mental escape hatch – I imagine he would feel a warm glow. I hope he knew this in his lifetime.

Duly distracted, Josh is temporarily lost to me; I can barely get a word out of him now. A granny-age volunteer appears by my side. I am such a foreigner to hospitals that I have no idea what a 'volunteer' actually is or does. Someone who doesn't get paid to be there, err... I have so much to learn about hospitals. She seems to be there to be moral support for me. She knows nothing about Josh or what we are doing, which at the time seems kind of weird; she asks me what he is 'in for'. I manage to stutter out 'they think he has leukaemia' and start sniffling. She is gorgeous, a bit like a friend's mum, hands me tissues and doesn't really know what to say, but stays by my side. We both start talking to Josh which makes it slightly less weird. This is an excellent technique, I learn over time – if you don't know what to say to the adult you are with, deflect everything to your child! Works a treat.

I am given a white coat, blue shoe covers and a hairnet. I have worn this exact same outfit in what feels like a previous life, visiting organic food production facilities in Oregon as a single, travelling Londoner. I reel inwardly at how strange life is; if someone had told me a decade ago while I watched blueberries being turned into puree that I would be wearing the same outfit while my middle child was being knocked out in order to put some weird tubing inside his chest and take out some of his bone marrow...I am lost for words. In the pre-operating theatre bit, which is sort of like an airlock on a spaceship, they ask me lots of questions confirming who he is, connect a huge syringe of what looks like toothpaste to his surfboard arm (after this operation he can chuck the surfboard out the window if he wants, yesssss), and reach to take the ipad from him as they ask him if he feels sleepy. "WHAT?!!" he shouts joyously, for the first time since Tuesday morning he is properly amused, "I NEVER go to sleep in the daaaaa......" He is out. They gently, so gently catch his lolling head and all, me included, laugh in a really loving, sweet way. Everyone is really human and, well, nice. My laugh turns into a weird kind of sob.

You place such immense trust in these people. An evil, demonic voice in my head starts along the lines of, "What if they get the anaesthetic dosage- What if something goes- What if an air bubble-" NO. Shut. It. Down. This is a choice, you can go down that path of anxiety or you can choose to worry about the things which really deserve it. The fact that he has leukaemia: cause for anxiety. The skill level of the people who are going to be saving his life: not a cause for anxiety. They have been learning, studying, training, practising and perfecting for years and years to do this thing which they do every day, this is a children's hospital with the most technologically advanced kit and skilled people, he is in the right place. Upgrade that: he could not be in a better place. I speak to my own brain emphatically. Internalise this: he is in the Right Place. We are so very, very lucky.

I also have a slightly weird ongoing thing inside my head about the doctors as, like Lawrence-Nick-Rob, they just all seem so damn familiar to me. Several of them talk to me about doing a few years in the big London hospitals when they hear my English accent, and plenty of my UK medic friends have done their stints in Australia too. In some areas we can speak the same language, a level frame of reference, if not medically. This helps, it helps immensely with the trust and shutting down the evil little voice of worry. I am hit by a sudden intense pang of longing that my friend Nick might appear round the next corner in a hospital corridor, white coat over his scrubs, broad smile, warm heart, telling me everything will be fine…what I would give to have a truly familiar friend in this foreign, frightening world. I haven't spoken to him for a few years, but I text him immediately and tell him.

I realise that my overexcitement about the similarities of the doctors to my old friends is probably the result of my brain desperately straining and reaching for reassurance wherever I can conjure it up. But this awareness doesn't diminish the potential power of it, I'm still going to choose to take comfort from these mental links, however tenuous the threads may be. As we walk this path, I am going to choose to find comfort and joy wherever I can, and to pass that on to Josh. Much later, a few months after Josh finishes treatment, Scott and I discover an incredible movie called Collateral Beauty. Its message is exactly what this realization is: I must be sure to notice the collateral beauty. And each beautiful moment will become a patchwork piece of the rich, gilded fabrics that make up my Gratitude Cloak. They will be my own personal version of the poet W. B. Yeats' 'heaven's embroidered cloths', a poem I loved so much in a past, much younger life phase when, in my age-appropriate naivety, I never dreamed those cloths would be anything other than a yearning for romantic love. Now they are the yearnings that my child will survive this. Tread softly, Fate.

So Josh is immediately wheeled out of sight, and two people take my elbows kindly and efficiently, and guide me out of the room. I have literally no idea where I am. I peel off my various nets and coat and someone tells me where to go and when, for when he wakes up in Recovery, and the volunteer reappears and hands me tissues. I dab at my eyes self-consciously, I should be more teary. I thank her like an automaton, take a deep breath and turn away from Joshie in his operating theatre and down to the long ramp which pops you out at Starbucks on the ground floor. I am really conscious that this is the furthest I have been from him since this nightmare began at home. From the ramp you have a view of the entire atrium of the ground floor of the hospital, and as I start walking down the ramp I see the boys, Scott's mum and my mum walking in the entrance doors and looking around for me. This is it, this is really happening.

Scott had a once-in-a-lifetime meeting scheduled far in advance with an Australian media person for this morning. We discussed it briefly, the person he is meeting is a really big, famous name. Whilst he would of course understand if Scott rescheduled because his son had just been diagnosed with leukaemia, he also probably wouldn't be able to reschedule and that would be that. The potential project is huge and would be a real accolade for the business if they won it. Scott and I agree that he should keep the meeting date. I have two grannies to support me now, and Scott will come to us as soon as his meeting finishes. So he isn't there while Joshie is in theatre.

Scott and I wonder if we are stark-raving bonkers making these kind of decisions. It is still such early days in our leukaemia 'journey', but already I can see that there is only one way Scott is going to cope with all this: he has to be able to continue to look after his business and get the mental break from the oncology world. Even after the first two days he is panicking that if he is with me and Josh all the time 'we will literally go out of business and the whole family will be f*cked'. Of the two of us, I am the more tolerant of waiting, sitting, listening, delays, last minute changes. For Scott, days sitting in the hospital worrying about whether his business is suffering is only going to add stress, which will turn into stress for all of us. Plus he is already juggling the day to day challenges of his spinal issues with the practicalities of commuting into the CBD and working in a professional office environment. And I work freelance for myself editing and proof-reading, which I can usually do after the boys are in bed. I am the one with the flexibility.

The grannies, the boys and I sit in the hospital café. I breastfeed Albie. Every single passing hospital staff member smiles at me; this is one heck of a breastfeeding-friendly environment. The wonderful grannies bring me hot chocolate, try to get me to eat. Ollie is happy and calm, reveling in any opportunity to be the grown up, responsible grandson; carrying hot drinks, getting napkins, all with a beautiful 'I am so grown up' expression on his tiny skinny face. I can't remember much about what we said. I try to bring them up to speed but the pace at which we are being given information means things tumble out of me in the wrong order and I doubt I make much sense. This is going to be a pattern; I have to find a better way of keeping everyone up to date.

After forty minutes I leave them to find Josh in the recovery ward. This is just horrible. I had seen Scott in recovery after his surgeries and knew to brace myself, but when it is your tiny child on a full size, raised hospital bed with safety bars up and tubes coming out of him...oh this is something else. Recovery is this huge, silent, white room, enormous, with a couple of silent nurses writing, observing, typing, adjusting... I feel like I am in a sci-fi movie. Someone has stuck one of the Keep Calm posters on the exit doors, this one says, 'KEEP CALM AND EAT CHOCOLATE.' Yes, yes I will do that. Maybe not right now but that moment is most definitely approaching. Right now it might be more like 'keep calm and try not to throw up', but still.

Josh is curled up on his side in the fetal position and barely stirring. There is a big rectangular dressing on his neck which is soaked in bright red blood. His little chest is bare and I can see the big, bloody dressing covering his stark white central line – the dressing is transparent. They did it. They cut into my baby's beautiful perfect nut-brown body and stuck alien 'outside' things inside him, oh god. And they didn't cut into him and then discover that actually it was all a mistake, a sick joke, and everything was fine in there. I mean I knew they were going to do it, of course I did, but here is undeniable physical proof that he has leukaemia. I can't pretend any more. I feel so, so sad. He isn't really aware it's me so I stand there holding tight onto the bars on the side of his stupid big, high, sterile, too-white bed, unable to see any more through my silent, hot tears and just ache with the pain of it, for him, for me, for our little family. Oh man... A thousand heartbroken swearwords.

Also something weird must have happened with the cleaning antiseptic that they use to swab the skin before they operate because he has fluorescent pink stuff all over his back and head and in his hair, staining his scalp. At first glance I think it is blood but it isn't, it is chlorhexidine. This is the antibacterial squirty stuff at every door in the hospital which you rub on your hands. (It has the consistency of water, and I am still completely hopeless at de-germing my hands without squirting it all over the place – the floor, my clothes, Josh – how the staff do it I have no idea, I've watched and I still don't get it. I am clearly spatially (squirtily) dyslexic.) It honestly looks like someone dropped a bottle of the stuff all over him. I tentatively ask the recovery nurse what happened but she is none the wiser and not remotely concerned about this; I guess to a medical professional he just looks extra clean. But to me, this and all the bright red blood just add to his pitiful state, this is a horrible way to see your child. And he has only had this done to him, how parents cope when their child is in a car crash, or has huge surgery performed I do not know. He still has a cannula but the recovery nurse removes it while he is still groggy, and just to add another little surprise his vein squirts a lovely big arc of bright red blood across the white sheet and the rail when she pulls the needle out. She leaps back and quickly presses it with a cotton wool blob, it stops immediately, but it does mean the first thing he sees when he opens his eyes is blood all over the sheet. Nice.

He slowly comes round, is wheeled back to his room and food is brought. I had assumed after a GA he would feel sick, not have any appetite, be totally out of it all day, but no, here is my first lesson in paediatric oncology; unless something weird happens they generally seem to be back to normal, and I mean literally normal, within an hour or so of coming round. A friend later explains to me that 'Australia is amazing for anaesthetics', both the type of meds they use, the dosages and the way that it is administered all meaning that children can get on with their day pretty quickly. Again my mantra swims around my head: we are so lucky, we are so lucky… And I make a mental note to encourage one of our sons to become an anaesthetist – rewarding skillset, interesting sector and apparently pretty sweet cash. Then I feel guilty for thinking about money, how mercenary of me. At this point I don't care if all three of them are happy spliffheads living at the bottom of mummy and daddy's garden as long as they are all healthy and, not to put too fine a point on it, alive.

CHAPTER 6

Day 4

Back on the ward, we suddenly 'get' the central line: he is hooked up and beeping away with his antibiotics and fluids within about forty-five seconds of returning to his room, and he is completely oblivious, doesn't even realize he is attached to anything until he jumps off the bed to retrieve some fallen Lego. It is several hours before he asks sadly if he can look in a mirror and see his chest. A nurse helps me prepare for his reactions and tells him that lots of children like to come up with a name for them. Some kids call them their spaghetti. Their noodles. Josh settles on tentacles; he loves under the sea stuff (thank you David Attenborough and Octonauts in equal measure). Later they are renamed 'noodles not needles', and a couple of months in when he has completely accepted that his body has tubes dangling out of it, he just calls it his central line. The way that things become normal, the way that children live in the now, the matter-of-fact acceptance of How Things Are is mind-boggling. I feel sure that if it were me or Scott, or most of the adults we know for that matter, we would have 'down days' where we focused on how appalling it was having a central line, or long stretches of worry about everything that could go wrong with it, or just anger at how bloody inconvenient it is not being able to swim, or lie back in a bath, or have a shower, or roly-poly down a grassy bank. (Because obviously Scott and I spend a lot of time roly-polying down grassy banks...)

At one point the grannies take Josh and his 'pole' (the pole on wheels with his intravenous stuff hanging off it, which connects to his central line) out of his room for a walk to the ward playroom with the brothers. Scott and I set them up and then walk down the ward on our own to grab five minutes of just us two. This is obviously noticed immediately by the staff, possibly via the afore-mentioned cctv cameras, a message is conveyed, and within seconds our oncology god swoops in on us while he can catch us on our own. This cannot be coincidence; it was literally the only time we were on our own in that first week. I am bowled over by how attentive the care is, how people are looking out for the parents, the siblings, the whole family from the sidelines without you being aware that you are being observed. This, to me, is care in the truest sense of the word. To be a part of this system, living in a country where this is what happens, is a massive, massive privilege. Every so often an image flits through my mind of a dinghy overloaded with Syrian refugees, mums holding babies...it is all happening right at this point in time and god I feel lucky. There are such horrific things going on, things that you are so far removed from but still make you cry into your pillow – the little Syrian toddler boy Alan Kurdi whose body was found washed up on a beach – and here we are in our own personal hell, living a parent's nightmare, yet so cared for, so supported. We are suffused with gratitude. It continues in this way.

We begin to be educated in the meaningful bullet points of what he has: ALL, the most common childhood cancer, the 'best' sort of leukaemia to have if you are going to have it, he is a 'good' age to have it, there is an excellent chance he will be completely cured. That said, nothing is certain yet, and now we begin to understand the wonder of science. Studies conducted every few years have honed and perfected the treatment schedule for kids with leukaemia so specifically that they can tell us precisely which days he will need bone marrow taken to measure what is happening, and these are seriously random days; numbers like 8, 15, 33... My mind is cast back to maths lessons and trying to spot patterns and predict the next number in a sequence. Not a chance.

We are handed a piece of paper with a really, really aesthetically un-pleasing diagram on it which needs some serious design help. It shows the path of treatment for the varying types of ALL, dividing them into different cell categories and then also different risk categories. I can just about pick out which trajectory we hope to stay on. Someone has decided it would be good to call some things by letters and other things by numbers, and some by combinations of both. To an oncologist this must be about as simple as reading a baby's 'That's Not My...' book. To me it is like an alien's language.

It's at this point, really early on in our learning curve, that I realize there is absolutely no point whatsoever in me googling. To this day, my mum cannot understand this, I am sure masses of friends can't either and would be staggered to know that I haven't ever typed 'Paediatric Acute Lymphoblastic Leukaemia' into google. I am fortunate to be educated, I am not afraid of long, complex scientific words (I love words, I love the origins of them, I can frequently be heard nerding out to my boys about the breakdown of modern words and what they stem from), and I like to get my head around things thoroughly and take them on. But! In this instance, these experts, these professors and doctors and nurses have such a depth of knowledge about a subject which is so foreign to anything I have ever studied that it seems insane even to attempt to crawl anywhere near their language. I am better off listening, absorbing, questioning, being educated solely by them. They provide exactly the right amount of information and education; not only has the treatment itself been researched and finely tuned, but so also has the way that they educate parents. They know how much to feed me, and when; they know what they are doing.

Besides, I am sure that google will provide me with whatever my mood steers me towards: if I am worried and I google, I will find my worries confirmed. If I am feeling positive and I google, I will find other happy stories. It is pointless. They don't explicitly tell me not to google or research anything, but they give us reams of papers and literature with the right kind of info to read, which is, crucially, generic. Again and again we are reminded that every child is different, every child responds differently to the chemotherapy, to the anaesthetics, to the steroids, to their own battle – some children knock it on the head, some children have exactly the same diagnosis and are not so fortunate. Some sail through the two year treatment with one or two unexpected brief hospital admissions, some have to stay as inpatients from the day they are diagnosed and experience every complication in the book. The internet will offer examples of all these, and without a tour guide to steer you towards facts which are truly relevant to your own child, it is too much for me to contemplate. In summary, I am too vulnerable for that.

My mum tentatively tries a few times to point out that there are online support groups for parents of children with exactly what he has. But I don't want to have digital relationships with strangers I will never meet who may have completely different emotional reactions to everything. I am about to encounter a lot of mums and a few dads during our many chemo trips and hospital stays, and these will form my actual real live human contacts for this horrible time. If they are only bound to me with one thing in common, our children's cancers, then that will be enough at the right moments. I have a feeling I will also want to be Just Me dealing with stuff for some of the time. So. No googling for me. If I have questions, I ask them and we get immediate, straight answers. I am told multiple times by different people that the standard practice in this particular hospital and for these particular oncologists is to be straight. You won't be told things are going well if there are not. Likewise you won't be given cause for alarm if there isn't a real reason. And when they don't have an answer they will tell you that they don't, and will tell you if and when you will get an answer. I like this. We have struck lucky, struck gold, with our people.

CHAPTER 7

Day 5

The first big shock is that treatment starts, like, yesterday. Every adult I have known who was given a cancer diagnosis had tests, scans or biopsies, had to wait days for results and answers, then probably a few more days to be given an idea of what next (surgery or straight into chemo or radio), and then a few more days before actually starting. Then, in one close friend's case who shared her experience with me, as soon as everything kicked off she was given a schedule of sorts spanning the upcoming months, with a dose of chemo every three weeks or so. Blood counts had to recover and be strong enough to withstand the next dose. So paediatric cancer is a little bit different...

It turns out that children's bodies can tolerate much more aggressive treatment than adults. In fact our oncology god even tells us that some of the doses in several of the protocols (Josh's treatment is divided up into chunks, basically segregated by the type of drugs which are administered, and these chunks are called protocols) would be fatal if given to an adult. Fatal. When he says this I feel a very peculiar mix of pride and horror. And awe, awe of children's strength. Apparently it is to do with how quickly they are growing and developing, how quickly their cells regenerate and grow. I look at my face in the mirror while brushing my teeth that night and instead of thinking negative stuff followed by 'but basically ok for forty', this time I see a face which is slowly and inexorably slowing down. Ha, thanks oncology god! How vain, how ridiculously irrelevant. But I have to have these daft slightly irreverent thoughts to get myself through I think. I don't intend to turn into a somber, always-serious freak overnight. I am still me.

Anyway, as it turns out, treatment literally did start yesterday. While he was under GA (general anaesthetic) having his central line put in, they also gave him a shot of chemo straight into his spine, just to kick off the fight. I learn a new word: intrathecal, shortened to IT. This means 'directly into the spinal fluid'. From now on, almost every time he gets a GA he also gets a lumbar puncture to give him one of these. The site of a lumbar puncture is, by the way, dressed with a tiny band aid about one inch square. That's it. Usually they use band aids with Kung Fu Panda printed on them. Good fighting vibes!! The band aids fall off in the bath. Josh didn't realize he had ever had one until he'd had about five and saw the panda floating around in the bath and asked what it was. A bone marrow gets a little blob of cotton wool stuck down with some extra sticky tape, also tiny and also falls off in the bath.

After a couple of days in hospital Scott and I decide we need to tell our friends in one fell swoop what has happened, and of course for our clunky generation this information-distribution honour falls to Facebook. We set up a closed group and here is what we post:

'On Tuesday our little Joshie was diagnosed with leukaemia. He has Acute Lymphoblastic Leukaemia (ALL). We are told this has a great cure rate of 95%+, but noone knows what is ahead and this is the beginning of a very tough journey.

We have set up this group as we are lucky to have lived in different parts of the world and still have close friendships with people who we don't see regularly, but who we feel are very much part of our lives. Scott or I will plan to put little updates (shorter than this) here from time to time to let you know how Joshie is doing.

For those who I haven't managed to reach yet: Joshie, our tough little lion, had a fever, no other symptoms, which we were keeping at bay with the usual panadol and nurofen, and when it didn't respond to antibiotics after 7 days the GP ran routine blood tests to rule out various things. We were setting off for the school run when the results came through and I had a call telling me to drive straight to Emergency. And everything changed.

For the moment we are of course absolutely shellshocked. On Monday I was snivelling while reading an emotional facebook post about a parent whose child was sick, thinking there but for the grace... on Tuesday afternoon that mummy was me. I am ricocheting wildly from a heap on the floor to steely mummy and wife.

A last thought - before this began I often found myself almost panicked about how bleak and horrible today's world can seem. Well we are only a couple of days into this, but already we have felt a deluge of warmth and love on a personal level from friends, family and strangers. Good comes from bad. And that is what is going to get us through this.'

The comments and responses are next level. I read them every night for weeks, no exaggeration, after Josh falls asleep and I am exhausted and have nothing left. I commit some to memory. It is like pouring, one by one, cups of clean, clear water back into an empty bucket, steadily filling up the clanging, dry void with thirst-quenching goodness. The goodwill spans the globe. Sydney to Montana to London to Washington DC to Geneva to Rome to Singapore to Abu Dhabi to Christchurch to Barcelona to Toronto... on and on the list goes, weaving a web of goodwill, vibes, prayers, lit candles in Catholic churches, well wishes wrapping up the globe in a cobweb mesh of love, human love. We care, say the comments on Facebook, shining out through my too-bright phone screen as I hold it in bed, we've got you. My bucket fills up, I fall asleep warmed by the bright, glowing flames of love. I am suffused with gratitude.

* * * *

We stay in hospital for seven days. This feels extraordinary to me, to all of us, but over the following weeks and months I meet so many parents whose initial admission lasted weeks and weeks, months even (one woman stayed with her daughter every night for four and a half months), that I feel immensely lucky. During our seven days Josh is treated for the infection that was causing the fevers. What this infection was is still a mystery, but now that I have a basic understanding of blood counts I know that when Chris from the pathology lab called me on that horrible Tuesday morning, Josh basically had no immune system at all, nothing. Anyway it doesn't really matter if we can't identify the source of the infection, it was a wonderful stroke of luck that he got whatever it was, as it steered us in the direction of getting him fixed. Besides, with no immune system he could have picked his nose and eaten it (highly likely for this beautiful child) and become horribly unwell. So as well as being given the intravenous antibiotics through his central line to nuke the infection, he also begins Protocol 1A.

Going from normal family life to Protocol 1A is full on; they kick it all off with a veritable onslaught of chemo, with huge doses of powerful steroids taken orally three times a day as a kind of 'backdrop' to the chemo. This combination wages an all-out war on the cancer cells, and the aim is that by the end of this protocol, after thirty-three days, the body will have been slammed into remission. And then on Day 34, the next brutal protocol begins for another few weeks with different back to back chemo meds, consolidating the remission, and when that protocol finishes, the next one begins, equally heavy, and so on for seven intensive months if all goes smoothly. After that we will go into eighteen months of what is called maintenance chemo – literally maintaining his body with more less intensive chemo in the most optimal way to prevent the leukaemia from rearing its head again. It is going to be a marathon.

So when I think about reaching Day 33, when the word 'remission' will hopefully be used, I am confused about how I will be expected to feel – when adult friends fighting cancer were told they had 'gone into remission' it was a moment of celebration, a tentative champagne moment, but it seems that for us that day will be more a case of 'right, we won the first fight, now we pick up a new sword and attack the enemy from a different vantage point'. There is definitely a Trojan Horse metaphor to be made here, chemo attacking leukaemia cells from the inside out, the warrior medicine delivered by wonderful nurses and doctors and a wonderful healthcare system, but unlike the sneaky horse the medical team and system truly are wonderful. We do not need to fear these Greeks bearing gifts. With apologies to Virgil, non timeo Danaos et dona ferentes!

Side effects for Protocol 1A are a baptism of fire. Holy moley there are many.

Some of the non-chemo medications that he has to take will prevent things happening in the first place, for example his blood counts will be suppressed by the chemo drugs for such a long time that there will be times when he basically has no immune system, is neutropenic. For this reason he takes an antibiotic to prevent chest infections for the entire two year treatment plan. But this particular antibiotic has its own side effects, whoo hoo! It will make him burn in the sun really quickly, so he is supposed to wear long sleeves and long trousers and a hat. For two years. In Australia. I glance around at the kids on the ward and in the clinic – all in shorts and t shirts. Hmm.

Also, a slightly crushing moment, we learn that all his vaccinations are gone, he has zero immunity to anything. Once treatment is finished, children are fully vaccinated to bring them back up to date with the schedule. That'll be a fun day, "Here are, oh, twenty-seven vaccination needles for your enjoyment, where shall we begin, a little bit of Tetanus perhaps, or maybe a meaty three course MMR bonanza…?" (Actually it was just five, with a cheery nurse on each side of him and an almost poetic symmetry to the well-practised rhythmic procedure: one - switch syringes – two – switch – and one-for-luck and all done, high fives, and intense gratitude that we live in an age where this is possible and he is once more protected.)

The steroids have lots of horrible side effects. Our nurse communicates this with a sort of raised eyebrows, tucked-in-chin expression, basically her entire face is managing to shout the words 'it's a bit shit' without her having to verbalise them. So this particular steroid, prednisone, is a regular word we are familiar with from asthma management, but it turns out that in enormous doses it does something fantastically destructive to cancer cells, so that when combined with the chemo onslaught the leukaemia is booted into remission. But of course it does a lot of things to small children, as well as to the cancer cells. It makes them ravenously, furiously hungry all the time, often for salty junk food. I am told to brace myself for constant demands for chicken nuggets. Scott mentally does an ecstatic little jig at the thought of having a genuine reason to go to the McDonalds Drive-Thru on a regular basis without me pursing my lips (my background, pre-Scott, is in the organic wholefood sector. McDonalds was kind of like swearing). Pred, as we start to call it pretty quickly, also causes 'steroid rage'. One child on the ward famously became so possessed with fury that he tried to rip out his own central line and had to be restrained by four nurses. Josh is really physically strong; this bit makes me nervous. The nurses talk to me quietly about finding my physical strength and being ready to restrain him should I need to. So the psychological impact, the rage, combined with the ravenous hunger means that you can forget any parenting aspirations you have of wholesome diets; if he asks for it during Protocol 1A, give it to him. He will need the extra weight in the months to come when he could get incredibly skinny and weak. And then the pred also causes fluid retention, in a big way. So that, coupled with the enormous unnatural appetite, means your child goes really quickly from the little bod you know, to a very, very different-looking person. Some children get stretch marks on their tummies as the skin is stretched so fast.

And there is no nice way of saying this: prednisone tastes really, really disgusting. I mean, imagine the most bitter thing you have ever tasted, say, maybe if you have accidentally chewed down hard on a cardamom pod in a decent curry. Or if you have accidentally licked the stuff that people paint on their nails to stop them biting them. Bitter aloes. Then intensify and magnify that bitter taste by about ten billion squillion, and that is what prednisone tastes like. And they have to take it three times a day. You have just about recovered from the trauma of getting them to take a dose, when it is time for the next. Seriously, for most of Protocol 1A Josh was either furious that he had to take his steroids in a couple of hours, or fighting tooth and nail not to take them.

For the first two days on the ward the nurses gave it to him as a syrup in a syringe. This was ghastly. And heartbreaking. It felt like every last vestige of control had been stolen from him, and now here were essentially strangers, kind ones, but strangers, waving a big fat revolting syringe right in his face telling him he just had to take it. They are experts at this, they know every trick in the book. A heavenly nurse came up with a plan to give it to him as a crushed tablet instead (well, several crushed tablets, they don't make tablets big enough for these doses), and then it could be mixed with something, in our case vanilla ice cream. This was fractionally less traumatic; at least this way he could choose where he was when he took it, what sort of spoon he wanted, whether he wanted a chaser of some sort (we went through jelly snakes, salt and vinegar crisps and settled on cheap and nasty peperoni sausage snacks for a while – anything with a really strong taste) and he could wrestle back a tiny bit of control of his own body.

After a few days in hospital Scott and I were so wrung out and upset by the drama involved, three times a day, in getting him to take this that we tasted the stuff ourselves to see what all the fuss was about. We had a newfound respect for Josh that he actually ever took it at all. Your entire mouth sort of recoils in shock like a separate part of your body, reproachfully telling your brain no, no, what…why…?? It was truly rank.

And the steroids are so strong that you need to protect the lining of the stomach from them, so there is another tablet to do that, a pink one in this case, which thankfully dissolves in water but makes the water taste like a murky pond.

In the shocked peace after one particularly awful medication-administering session in the hospital where both Scott and I almost exploded in a puff of blue smoke and Joshie reached breaking point and had to be stopped from running away down the corridor 'because I HATE you!!!', my phone pings. Before this all began we had been in the process of setting up a vegetable garden; we had built three raised beds and were about to fill them with soil and plant the beginnings of our country life. On my phone is a message and a series of photos. Unbeknown to us, while we are up here in the hospital a little group of our closest friends has been toiling away in our garden. One of the huge raised beds is full of soil, mulched and planted out. It looks beautiful. I gasp and burst into tears. I hold the phone up to Scott and he also gets really teary; this is kindness on another level. The accompanying message from our beautiful green goddess friend says that they all decided Joshie was going to need plenty of nutritious organic food to help him fight his upcoming battle and so they have made the start for us. We are absolutely speechless with love, surprise and emotion. At such a horrible, all-consuming time, to be faced with such immense altruism and support – it is like being thrown a life buoy (which our boys inexplicably insist on calling a 'life-ty buoy', merging 'safety' and 'life') to grab onto: "Here, grab this lifeline! You are going to survive! We are here, we're going to rescue you!" Actually forget the life-ty buoy, this was like having a full-size coastguard boat pull up alongside us and announce, "Climb on! We can get you through the storm!" We are living in the best community. What fantastic people. Surely this is the very definition of community; people coming together to give support. And what staggers me is that they just did it – they knew not to ask 'would it be alright if' or 'what kind of vegetables'; they were confident in their wonderful, wonderful plan and executed it astonishingly. Such beautiful humans. The support continues in other ways as the weeks and months tick by. Truly we are riding with the coastguard.

CHAPTER 8

Day 10

We are discharged and sent home with a stash of steroids, 'the pink tablet', the antibiotics and the anti-emetics to stop him vomiting after chemo. Thankfully the anti-emetic is available as a 'magic wafer' – these are phenomenal. The tiny white wafer pops out of a regular pill packet and dissolves almost instantly on his tongue. We will be back in a couple of days for the next iv chemo.

Leaving hospital is terrifying on so many levels. We have been metaphorically cocooned in our new world of supportive people, and literally cocooned in psychedelic Australian animal curtains for a week. I know that returning to our home, our cats, our garden is going to be incredibly hard as well as fantastic. When we left that house, we were setting off to school on some idle Tuesday. The garden, which we inherited from the previous owners and can take no credit for, is an absolutely stunning Spring garden. They used to open it to the public and won awards in previous years. From the first day of Spring it explodes into a riot of champagney blossom and colour; the most enormous crabapple tree welcomes you like a giant's candy floss on a stick as you drive in, frothy ornamental plums and peaches line the driveway, irises, snowball bushes, quince, laburnum, aquilegia, tulips, honesty, lilac, weeping cherry, bluebells, hyacinths, and later roses and hydrangea… they are all there. When we drive in our gates this will all be in full celebratory bloom, but nothing will be the same. Nothing will ever be the same again. I feel so daunted, heavy-hearted with apprehension at the thought of how this is going to feel. One nurse tells me surreptitiously to pour myself a big glass of wine once we are unpacked and the boys are in bed. I don't have the heart to tell her I don't drink.

And on a practical level, this is where life is about to change completely. I am armed with a medication chart to stick on the fridge showing what he takes and when. I have a big purple bag with 'CYTOTOXIC' in big letters on it full of spare equipment for his central line dressing in case it has to be changed unexpectedly before his next appointment. We are educated extremely thoroughly in the details of chemotherapy, namely that for 7 days after Josh has received a dose his body is still excreting it through any means possible – tears, sweat, vomit, wee, poo, saliva… he himself is toxic to the rest of us. This is properly weird and scary. I have to wear disposable hospital gloves for cleaning up anything that comes out of him. All his wee and poo, and preferably vomit, MUST go down the loo – little-boy-splashes of cytotoxic wee on the floor are not ok.

We are told that if we have more than one bathroom, he should use one exclusively, and the rest of the family should use the other one. As it turns out, we have one small family bathroom and a little ensuite off our bedroom which we don't use, as the survey said it had leaky pipes when we bought the house a year ago. We've been meaning to do something about it and haven't got round to it. And now we are the recipients of another act of off the scale kindness: we call a friend who has a building company and ask him to come and quote to fix it. He turns up on the same day despite his jam-packed schedule, pencil behind his ear, all heart, big workboots and capable hands, takes a look, somehow magics a small team of builders out of thin air and they just sort it out, refusing any payment. We have a bathroom for Joshie. We stumble to find the words to express our gratitude, I feel so humble, so intensely human in the face of such pure, genuine kindness.

I make a mental note to go out and buy several cans of hospital grade disinfectant to place at various points around the house. We usually use planet-friendly cleaning products but I haven't got the guts to ask the medical team if there are any eco cleaning options lest I be branded 'that hippy mum who hasn't got a clue what she is dealing with'. Not that anyone we have met would be so unkind; I think they have seen it all frankly, this is the least judgmental group of humans I have ever encountered. I am also given a huge stash of hospital vomit bags. One bulk pack for the glove compartment in the car, a stash for the house, one for under his pillow, one for my handbag… This is all feeling very scary, exactly how much vomit are we about to be flooded with?

We have reams and reams of paperwork and booklets to put on the coffee table in the sitting room. We have forms to fill in to apply for help with the cost of driving up and down to the hospital several times a week for his chemo. Forms to fill in in case we want to stay at the Ronald McDonald House attached to the hospital as we live far away (note to self: don't be so mean about McDonald's, they will have a part to play in this story and you will want everyone who you know to go there and buy a burger and some socks to help fund the incredible, incredible Ronald McDonald House Charities).

I discover that right from the outset we were a 'red flag' to the care team for three reasons:
1. We have a baby
2. Scott's spinal cord injury
3. We live far away
Each of these factors on their own would be enough to mark you out as a family who need extra support.

I'm not sure whether living ninety minutes away is a good thing or a bad thing actually. Sydney people roll their eyes in sympathy when they hear where we live, but then in the next breath they describe their own journeys taking almost an hour sitting in stationary traffic to travel a few kilometres. (Sydney is notorious for its traffic, although being British, I can't help thinking that people who complain about it clearly haven't ever sat on the North Circular at rush hour in London... Or the M4 on a bank holiday. Or the M25, like, ever.) But apart from the time involved, I have to say I like that we can completely remove ourselves from each world if we need to. If we have an overwhelming day at the hospital we can get in the car and drive through beautiful countryside, full of soul and history, to our relatively rural home. When we are up at the hospital, we are truly geared up for it, in the parallel universe. I am aware that I'm scrabbling to find silver linings, and there are times when it is too exhausting to drive home, but in those instances we are also terrifically lucky to have loving, warm-hearted inlaws with open arms and comfy bedrooms only half an hour from the hospital. When it's too tiring we just don't drive home until the morning.

Back home, one of the most daunting things to adjust

to mentally is the Action Plan. This I laminate and stick on the fridge. (Yes, I have a laminator, even though I am not a school teacher. Yes, this goes against my 'use less plastic' goals, but when it comes to paediatric oncology some things just have to be laminated.) So basically the rule for any child with cancer is that if they get a fever of 38 degrees or higher, you get to Emergency as quickly as you can, because they cannot fight any infection so it can become life-threatening extremely quickly. Once at Emergency they need to be connected to antibiotics within sixty minutes of arrival. When they have been afebrile (fever-free) for forty-eight hours you can go home. But the minimum admission would be forty-eight hours. Non-native English speakers are given laminated red and white cards saying 'oncology patient: requires urgent assessment and treatment' to hold up as they walk in.

(A little side note on non-Native English speakers. During our initial stay on the oncology ward I couldn't work out why half the signs were written in French as well as English. It turns out that there is no oncology care in New Caledonia, and the Australian government has an agreement with the French government (New Caledonia is a French territory) to treat their children with cancer. Very civilized. There is a lot that is wrong with modern-day government, but learning this did make me stop and appreciate the good stuff. If people can use civility, kindness and common sense at that high a level, then surely there is some hope for the human race.)

And so we arrive home. It is somehow awful and normal at the same time. I begin to feel a dull, depressing feeling in my stomach; there is no escaping the enormity of our reality. Maybe this is the beginning of acceptance. I keep getting a sort of psychological prickling in my brain, angry, spiky words: 'But I don't want this.' It's spiky and angry, but ultimately it's just whining. I cannot do anything about it, I can't change things, it just is, this is how it is. And even after a week it is still unbelievable. In fact coming home makes it all the more so – are you serious? Is this for real? One friend writes on our facebook page, 'It seems inconceivable that this is happening to you, but it is.' That kind of sums up my brain for about 90% of the time at this point. (Despite the fact that any time I see the word 'inconceivable' I say it in a Princess Bride voice. It is the perfect word though, an apt word, for those struck by trauma and tragedy. A friend's wife died: it is inconceivable. How, how can this be?)

As we unpack the car, the cats look at us with their usual schizophrenic disdain / adoration. The garden looks greener and more colourful than ever before to my hospital eyes. My bed, oh my bed! It is like lying on a cloud! A huge, cool, smooth, cloud of familiarity. The boys race straight to their toys, their Lego, their 'friends' (the ten billion soft cuddly toys which threaten to engulf their bunk beds), and within minutes are constructing something and arguing about who will get to play with it first. Albie crawls around shouting joyfully at everything in recognition – ah! My highchair! Ah! A shoe! Ah! The apple remote, I have missed this! Delicious! It is all very normal. But it is all so horribly different.

One thing that stands me in good stead is that I am someone who takes great pleasure in getting organized. I unpack, throw things in the washing machine, get out the Redkite cancer diary, choose a spot for his medications, I clear space on the fridge to stick the important stuff up. I add every new essential name to my phone with detailed notes about who they are, what they can help with, their pager numbers (I don't even know how pagers work, do you dictate a message, what if it is a long message? I later discover the best option is 'Please call Joshua Hammond's mum not urgent thank you'. Absolute rocket science).

By now Ollie has had a week off school. Australia is good about this; his wonderful school just understood and sent the most incredible message of support offering any assistance we might need. So now he needs the reassurance and comfort that seven year olds get from a return to routine and normality.

Our logistical plan from this point onwards is complex and takes all my strength to work out. Once finally organized I feel like I deserve some letters after my name, maybe a phd in spreadsheet and logic nerd studies. It frankly takes so much brain power that I have hardly any energy left for fear or anxiety about what is actually happening at this point, so I'm actually really grateful. In fact this applies to plenty of other facets of the experience; getting him to take his medicines is one of the worst parts of it, staying organized, expecting the unexpected – there's no choice about whether or not I sort it all out, this stuff all HAS to be done. It adds strange layers of stress and worry. It kind of feels like there's this massive underlying Awful Thing, the leukaemia obviously, and then layered on top of that are all the individual stresses that come with it, because of it, and then on top of those are the everyday things which are just part of normal life anyway – paying bills, not running out of nappies, remembering to put the bins out... Feeding the family looms large in my mind, how on earth am I going to find the time, the headspace, dammit the ability even to cook meals for us all when we are in different places at different times? Looking at our chemo schedule we will often be coming home knackered at the end of the day, and the prospect of trying to get the three boys fed, bathed and to bed makes me want to cry. Even on a normal, pre-leukaemia day this is such a bunfight, as it is for so many families: breastfeeding Albie, reading the boys a story ("Two each mummy?

Pleeeeeease? What if they're reeeally short ones?"), getting everyone a drink of water, giving in to bedtime bananas (yes you will have to brush your teeth again) because how can you say no when they are skinny, invariably supervising a bum-wipe because OBVIOUSLY this was the optimal moment to do a poo, it goes on and on, as every parent knows. But now factor in the fact that one of them is terrifyingly sick, will need to be taking medicine at bedtime, might do a massive toxic-vomit at any moment...I finally understand the millennial phrase that has up until now bemused me: I can't even.

Then something happens which makes me almost faint with gratitude, firstly, and then makes me cry. A friend emails saying several of them had got together to brainstorm ways they could help us, significantly and effectively. They get that it is really hard to identify what kind of help you need, and often incredibly hard to ask, so they have come up with a list of stuff which may be totally off the mark or may be helpful. I am given the option to say 'yes please', 'maybe' or 'no f*ck off'. I love this, as well as bowling me over with kindness , the 'f*ck off' option also really makes me laugh, I love that they are not tiptoeing around me. These are people who are clearly extremely highly qualified in putting themselves in someone else's shoes, however horrible the shoes are.

Among the fantastic offers is the heavenly 'Arrange a dinner roster'. And so the Dinner Ladies are born. Lots of friends begin to send messages telling me to let them know if there is anything they can do to help. So I take a deep breath and instead of thanking them and saying I'll let them know (when I finally do get round to replying, which is hard as you have to have the headspace to feel like typing and forming sentences, and also not be so tired that you can't actually type, and also not be crying) I tell people that actually a friend is forming a list of people who might be able to cook us the odd meal. I have to be brave about this as it feels selfish actually saying 'actually yes please' instead of just thanking them for the sentiment, but it is time to grow up a bit in that regard. The response is incredible. Within days we have thrice-weekly drop-offs. With no allergies and no headspace for fussiness (and a little boy on pred who is basically turning into a walking chicken nugget by this point, all my fears were confirmed) we fall on the lasagne, spag bol, chicken pesto pasta, pies, pizzas... It is like eating delicious mouthfuls of pure unadulterated support; I can feel the empathy and concern in the little notes each friend leaves with their meals, and I am certain that the health benefits of this kind of support extend way beyond the nutritional. Some of the Dinner Ladies are close friends, some have simply heard our news and just want to do something to help. I derive massive, massive strength from this. My little 'thank you' texts don't come close. I ponder over ways we can ever express our gratitude – a huge party at the end of all this if we have a good outcome. With a jumping castle and a massive barbecue and caterers. Because we will have won the lottery by then obviously (actually on that note I had a great conversation with another mum on the ward recently where she said ever since her beautiful one year old was diagnosed with the same thing as Josh they had started buying lottery tickets. If you can be the one who gets leukaemia, you could also be the one who wins the lottery.)

The only other time in my life when meals have just appeared out of nowhere was in Abu Dhabi when Scott had his spinal cord injury. We had up until then shied away from employing a live-in maid. Every one of our friends thought we were certifiably insane; this is one of the main reasons that many families choose to live there, the affordable, lovely help with the home and the kids. I just could never get my head around the 'us and them'-ness of it. I would have been a hopeless employer; I would have wanted everyone to be friends, and I am told that is not the right, respectful way to manage the relationship. Plus you are responsible for their residency visa, and the money you pay them is usually sent straight back to the Philippines or Sri Lanka (where almost all the domestic maids in the UAE come from) to support their own children who are brought up by the grandparents. We were living there on a comparatively tight budget while Scott set up his own company, unlike almost everyone else who was employed by international or local companies – it's no place for start-ups unless you're in fast food, or something where you get paid at the point of purchase. So this meant that we never really knew how long we would be living there, and could never have comfortably taken on responsibility for another human's welfare. So we had gorgeous girls from a cleaning agency who helped with the housework, and then after Scott's injury a friend leant us her maid who cooked incredible Sri Lankan food for us. I would take the then-tiny boys down to the beach, and we'd come back to find warm bowls of mildly curried shredded beetroot, little round flatbreads, or aromatic creamy butter chicken in my kitchen, and a spotless countertop. It was heaven.

And so are the Dinner Ladies. A fantastic friend who owns a removals company finds us a spare fridge-freezer which we set up outside the back door, and the Dinner Ladies put the food straight in there in foil trays which I can put straight in the oven and then rinse and put in the recycling bin. It is humbling, and it is no exaggeration to say this extreme kindness is probably the main thing which enables me to cope. It is so much more than just food.

CHAPTER 9

So the logistics.

Scott will return straight away to his usual work routine of being up in Sydney a few days a week, my mum will base herself here with us and take on the role of keeping Ollie's life as normal as possible, and I will be with Josh for his appointments. Little Albie will be the roving entertainment, travelling to Sydney with me and Josh where Scott's parents can look after him while we're in hospital. In an emergency, if Josh 'spikes' to 38 or higher while we are at home, mum will stay with Ollie and Albie and our Sydney hospital team have arranged the care plan with our lovely local hospital so that we can be there in minutes. I also have a group of our closest friends on standby to grab Albie if we are out and about in our hometown.

The unpredictability of this is horrible. They prepare you for a tough scenario, maybe not the worst case scenario since I guess in paediatric oncology the worst case scenario is, to be blunt, death. Everything is set within that bigger picture, an unspeakably frightening backdrop which, as the weeks go by, I find I just have to live sort of 'alongside'.

Yes, no-one can tell us categorically that he is not going to die. No-one says those words you long to hear: 'it's all going to be ok'. I once made the mistake of saying to one of our nurses, 'no-one has ever told us that he will definitely be ok,' and got a reassuring, uplifting but still non-committal reply which made me feel even worse. I learnt my lesson: don't go fishing because you won't catch a big fish. You'll just get a crappy kind of mini sardine, an afternoon snack to keep you going, not a nice satisfying meal.

Although no-one on our immediate medical team tells us anything categorical, one extremely highly qualified surgeon who knows Josh's case does say something to his daughter and her husband (our great friends), and they report straight back to us. His words were: "It will be very tough, but they will make him better." Said slowly, emphatically. When she tells me I feel a massive wave of relief washing over me; it's weird how great the words sound when they are said out loud even if they're not being said by an oncologist. Another friend sends a message a few months in and ends with the words, "Joshie is going to be fine, Katie!" He isn't a medical person at all, he's an investment banker who loves clubbing and mind-altering substances, but in that moment I love his conviction.

So they prepare you for a pretty rough scenario, and once home, I resolve to grit my teeth and get organized, half-expecting him to get a fever that night just, well, because. I'm given our own thermometer, the same sort the nurses use in hospital, and told to take his temperature once a day (assuming he doesn't seem unwell), preferably at different times of day so you get a genuinely random picture.

I unpack the Redkite bag and re-pack it with everything Joshie and I will need for forty-eight hours in hospital: duplicate toothbrushes, toothpastes, travel sized everything, underwear, changes of clothes... As time goes by, and after our first unexpected admission, I tweak this and pack fewer peanut m&ms and more literature. There is a lot of sitting around and not much physical movement when you are a cancer mum. After losing about 5kg in the first week (it was probably more like 2kg but you start moving like you are rake-thin because your shoulders are hunched and your stomach is caving in because of the horror of it, and you therefore feel really thin and gaunt, which is kind of sickeningly thrilling in itself), I realize pretty quickly that if I continue shoving chocolate in my mouth 'to get me through this' and 'to give me an energy boost' I will swiftly turn into Obese Cancer Mum and possibly develop diabetes, neither of which will make me feel good. I need to modify the chocolate from 'any type' to 'only dark chocolate and really nice chocolate'. This is the kind of compromise I am prepared to strike when it comes to chocolate. I am not going to sit there feeling worried about Josh while only eating tofu and beans and trying not to fart, I am still going to eat things I like. Although having said that, tofu makes me think about yoga – I wonder if any cancer mums spend their inpatient times doing meditation and stretching on a yoga mat. This could only be a good thing surely, although I have a feeling other parents would think you were stark raving mad. And maybe just a little tiny bit annoying.

I go out and buy a cheap baby bag with a ridiculous number of pockets. This is my cancer mum bag. Cancer diary in one pocket, Josh's stuff in another, wallet, phone, keepcup, normal handbag stuff, emergency surprises (toy car, tiny stretchy rubber dinosaur, chocolate gold coin), rose quartz little guardian angel carving from a friend, crystals from another friend, sick bags, iphone charger, earl grey teabags, sunhat and bandana ready for his bald head. Yes, I am ready for this. Am I? Can I ever be?

These slightly OCD-level organizational tasks are getting me through these first days back home. I feel a sense of purpose while I am doing them, and a sense of achievement and satisfaction when they are done. This in turn makes me feel capable. And in the face of the unknown, where all you know is that the unknown is going to be really tough (whatever the hell that means), being as prepared as you can be feels good. I keep hearing my UK Army friend Harry's voice saying gleefully, "It's the five Ps! Prior Preparation Prevents Piss-poor Performance!" I can see his face when he says it, huge smile, sparkling brown eyes, he is life personified; apt for this life-death experience, "LIVE NOW! LIVE NOW!" he is shouting at me just by his very appearance. Inside my head. He doesn't have a clue that I am channeling him on the other side of the planet. Am I going mad?

It does this, the paediatric oncology thing. It seems, uninvited, to open up chasms in your memory and allow meaningful moments to spark through, however long-faded and distant they may be. A clever coping mechanism perhaps: your life's experiences up to this point are what will get you through. The psychological 'you got this' made manifest.

Going out into the normal world is seriously daunting. Shopkeepers still say, "Hi how are you?" brightly, Australia is very friendly like this. I fake it beautifully, smiling, "Good thanks how are you?" I start out in shops fractionally further from home in the next town, thinking I'm unlikely to bump into people. Then I venture into Target in my hometown where I promptly bump into someone I know from baby group who I haven't seen for weeks. She hasn't heard the news and I have to say it in Target. She starts crying. She is the first acquaintance I tell in a random place face to face, and I realise I am going to need to get used to people welling up when I tell them. I decide my strategy has to be warn them first that we have had bad news, keep it short, get going. But one of the best things about living in a small town and having a schoolboy, a preschooler and a baby who was born here relatively recently is that I have met plenty of people already, and pretty quickly they have all shared our news and I don't have to repeat it to fresh ears too many times. I wonder what it was like when the news first got out, the hushed, wide-eyed conversations in the playground at pick-up, have you heard, did you hear what happened to the Hammonds? I have to walk into that playground soon.

So I imagine that anyone who has been through something rough will identify with this next thing - I am tough as old boots in some ways, but it hits you at the weirdest times. I would not have picked the supermarket, but... We need milk and cat food, I'll dash in, get this first mundane supermarket visit out of the way. I always, always see someone I know in Coles; it is located exactly between preschool and school. But it's Sunday, I might be ok this time. I park, pull down my sunglasses and walk purposefully towards the trolleys. I don't need a trolley for my shopping but I do need one kind of like a shield. I dump my now-giant cancer mum handbag bag in it and grip the handle. Deep breath, you can do this. I glance at my bracelet: You've Got This. Steel. The tough half of me snorts with derision at the self-indulgence of Making A Fuss About Coles. Get a grip.

In we go, past a sausage sizzle at the front doors, cool. What a nice Aussie country town having a sausage sizzle, I think. I stare straight ahead at the fruit and veg, and the tannoy announces merrily, "Good morning Coles shoppers! There are ten minutes left for our sausage sizzle in the car park, come and buy a delicious sausage and help raise money for Redkite, the charity that supports children with cancer and their families!" and bam, I am a 6 foot tall teary wreck in the sweet potatoes. That's us, that's my son, 'Redkite', that's a word we hear in our other world at the hospital not a word for the fruit and veg section, a thousand swearwords, aagghhh..... Sunglasses down off my head, do the rest of the shopping in semi darkness, pretend I am just hungover.

Actually I almost spoke to someone. Part of me wishes I had. A tastefully-dressed middle-aged looking lady (there are many of this social-economic demographic in our hometown, it is a place with plenty of 'jolly nice people') catches my eye just as I well up. She has a naturally smiley face and her smile widens as our eyes meet – this is the kind of town where you smile at people on the street if you catch their eye. (How lucky are we to live here?! I have lived in a lot of different places both as a child and an adult and there are not that many places where strangers smile at each other, I will never take this for granted.) In that split second I almost begin, "Sorry...I...my son..." and then the moment is gone and I reach out and pick up a completely pointless sweet potato which I am not going to do anything with instead. We humans, we are so conditioned to Act Normal. Or maybe it's because I'm English; even though I don't shy away from open-heartedness, still I am conditioned to avoid the awkwardness – I would have made her feel awkward, and knowing that she was uncomfy would have made me worse and now I am spinning in a never-ending cycle of awkwardness. Just pick up the sweet potato.

Over time, the supermarket experience shifts and settles into a strange type of discomfort. I feel it in my shoulders, this crawling sensation that someone somewhere might be looking at you and they might know what you're going through, it's odd and very hard to describe. It's a sort of acute, sharp self-consciousness mixed with brittle fragility, a feeling that people might be staring, wide-eyed, if they recognize me and know what's happened, but mixed with the certainty that if anyone says anything nice or supportive I really might just start crying in the middle of the street. Which would then in turn make them die inside of awkwardness, and then I would feel guilty of ruining their morning and probably start apologizing – it's like a sort of overcomplicated emotional brick-laying: slap another layer of negative emotion on with a trowel. Again, that extraordinarily British deep vein running through the heart of me, that the worst thing you could do would be to make someone else feel awkward. I bet Americans don't have this, I bet they would waltz into the supermarket with their perfect straight white teeth and their sunny self-justification and just OWN the fruit and veg aisle no matter what drama was going on at home.

Four weeks before he was diagnosed, Joshie had had a bike crash. He'd left his bike right at the end of the garden the day before – actually scrap that, he had carelessly flung his bike next to the compost heap and the logpiles where the snakes and spiders throw parties – and he ran off without his helmet to retrieve it after preschool one day. He came pedaling furiously back across the bumpy grass and onto our drive which is covered in a fine, sharp, slightly red-coloured gravel. The gravel looks like those tiny sweets from the 1990s called Nerds which came in little 2-flavour boxes, tons and tons of berry-flavoured Nerds all spread out on the ground. So Josh comes hooning back, hits a tree root and goes absolutely flying over the handlebars, landing with full force on his cheekbone. I didn't see it but the screams were the sort where you drop everything and leg it – Ollie was white-faced and shouting his shocked retelling of the fall, Josh was beside himself, which I think is probably the only time in his life he has been like that. His cheek was pretty mashed up, but after cleaning out the gravel and making him pull lots of weird expressions (which bizarrely reminded me of my French teacher Miss Pope when I was at a posh girls' school in Manchester aged eleven, explaining that English people didn't move their faces when they talked, unlike the French who use every facial muscle – see it's just like they say, you never forget those teachers) I reckoned he didn't need to see a doctor, slathered antibiotic ointment all over it and dressed it in a huge white rectangle, which he hated.

Two days later it was massively swollen but not causing him any pain apart from on the skin, as far as I could tell. As it was properly vast and all the colours of the rainbow, and the GP didn't have any appointments available, I thought we'd pop into Emergency at the local hospital and see how busy it was. Maybe it was cracked and they would x-ray it. Well it wasn't busy, so feeling very sheepish and like a bit of an idiot-time-waster, we stuck around and saw a nice man who was the ER doctor on call. He was wearing what to me looked like extra-serious medical scrubs with all sorts of embroidered things on them which basically said 'extremely senior'. He looked like he had just saved a couple of lives before breakfast. Anyway it turns out he is one of the school and preschool dads, though I didn't know this at the time. He is a man of few words; after a friendly chat with Josh about how he also had sons about the same age, he ripped off the dressing unceremoniously and gave his cheekbone a good poke. He concluded there was nothing broken and it didn't need an x-ray, but prescribed antibiotics for the skin. I apologized profusely for being a patient who walked out of ER with a prescription you would get from the GP, and he was very nice about it. However, before he dismissed us he squatted down on the floor so his face was level with Josh and just stayed there for what seemed like ages, staring at his face and his eyes. Not a word, just stared at him seriously. Josh was cool as a cucumber and didn't find anything weird about this. Maybe this doctor does this with every patient and it is just his way. But a tiny kind of niggling voice in the very back of my head won't shut up, wants to know: did he suspect something? Did he know? I mean they didn't do any bloods or tests or anything, there is absolutely no reason he would have thought 'leukaemia', from what I know now, but I wonder. One day I will have the guts to collar him in the playground and say, "Oi! Man of few words, remember me, overly-apologetic time-wasting mum of son with grazed cheek?" (to which I have no doubt at all the answer would be a courteous, 'Err, nope.') "So did you, umm, maybe think he had leukaemia?" Hmm. How good would it be if there were people who could just scan you with their eyes and go, yep, early stage cancer… no, all clear… Now there's a movie plot.

The school playground terrifies me and also kind of beckons me in equal measure. I've got to face it, and I'm not going to vanish off the face of the planet for the next two years. I am still Ollie's mum and he still has to go to and from school, and if I'm at home it shouldn't always be Granny who takes him, he needs the consistency of mummy as well. In fact probably now more than ever before he needs the consistency of mummy.

I decide to get it over with sooner rather than later and leave Josh and Albie at home with mum at the first opportunity. As we drive into town we run through how he feels right now about Josh being ill, and what he could say if anyone asks him about it. My nightmare scenario is some well-meaning but ditzy mum (with a blank face, I can't actually picture anyone I know doing this) accosting him in the playground and saying too-loudly with pantomime-level pity, "Ooooh goodness how's your BROTHER?! Is he OK? You POOR THINGS!" Or a child from an older class saying something mean about 'cancer germs'. I have no idea where I get these ideas from, but the idea that little 7 year old Ollie could be put on the spot and upset by someone else's words terrifies me. I won't be there to protect him, I won't be there to shield him. He on the other hand is cool as a cucumber and just sighs and patiently says, "Mum I know what to say. Yes he is very sick but he has really really good doctors and everybody loves him." I decide to trust him at his word; he knows this is true as well, it's not a line we've told him and then gone round the corner and cried about. Ollie is going to be fine, and besides I can't stay and shield him from everything, and that wouldn't help him anyway. I have to choose to believe he is going to be fine.

Of course nothing like that happens. When it comes to the crunch people are generally awesome, and we are lucky to live in a community with a very high proportion of particularly awesome people.

We park in our usual spot, I pull my sunnies over my eyes, hold his hand probably a little bit too hard and march in. I've always done this thing with the boys when we're holding hands where I do three squeezes and whisper-chant, "I! Love! You!" and then they squeeze it back, and then I do it back without the words and so on until someone gets bored – they love it and think it is like a secret code that no-one else knows is happening. Ollie and I do this all the way into school along the path and into the playground. And then as we round the corner I remember: for some reason more of the parents in Ollie's class hang around at drop-off than from any other class. There is a little bunch of them, all lovely people, in a huddle and we cannot avoid them. I take a deep breath and smile brightly as we approach, and I see every face has the same expression, a sort of surprise mixed with horror and pity and uncertainty about what they are supposed to say to me. I hate this, I hate that people don't know what to say to me. I don't know what to say to me for god's sake! I don't want people to feel awkward. But I also realize in a snap-instant that I can't take on the role of making other people feel comfortable, it is enough for my mental health to keep myself functioning right now. I have to shelve that part of me which instinctively wants to make things less awkward, make things normal. It IS awkward and it ISN'T normal, and really, accepting that is going to be how I move forward. So we plough on, much as my feet want to do a 180 and run away, away across the grass, and then we are nearly upon them and a strange human thing happens. They quite literally move apart in one movement, leaning away from us physically out of an unspoken fear of crowding us I guess, and as a result we come to a halt standing in the middle of a ring. It is so ridiculously awkward, such an impossible social moment and not one of us knows what we are meant to do (apart from in my case I know I mustn't run away) that I burst out laughing, this is hilarious. We are Moses and the Red Sea has parted before us. Snort.

"Argh!" I laugh-yelp, breaking the weirdness, "You've made a circle around us!"

I think everyone tried to say something meaningful and not-flippant without crowding us. Every action, every sound was well-meant, there was nothing hostile or negative about it, just seriously weird and excruciatingly uncomfortable. Done, tick, out of the way.

It is a strange feeling, that sensation of knowing that people see you and feel for you, unsure whether they want to ask or they want to avoid...on a tired day it makes my shoulders slightly more hunched. I stand a little less tall as

I walk around town. I find myself speeding up in supermarket aisles if I see an acquaintance if I don't have the energy to tell the story or talk about it. This makes me sad; I love to stop and smile and talk to people I recognize, and actually also to strangers. One of the things I have always hoped is that despite my height I look approachable. People say how wonderful it must be to be tall and of course it has its advantages, but you are also by default quite literally looking down on people, so it is a constant battle not to appear supercilious or aloof. AND I have quite a long nose which adds to the caricature perfectly. Should I wish to appear aloof I need only tilt my head back twenty-five degrees, flare my nostrils slightly and bam – I am most certainly looking down on you. I bet this is a peculiarly female issue, I bet tall men don't worry about being aloof. They just stride along being tall, thinking about how flies can stand on the ceiling upside down and similar pressing issues that have a positive impact on the logistics of day to day family life.

So when I bump into people I know, I want to share and be friendly, but the exhaustion of being upbeat and repeating the phrases again and again is real. In the very early days there is a certain catharsis in saying it out loud, although it is mixed with a peculiar guilt that you are sharing negative news with someone whose day may be made that little bit less happy because of it. But as you begin to live with the 'realness' of it - he has leukaemia, it is no longer new news - repeating it becomes slightly formulaic. Formulaic but also somehow never less shocking, even to me and to Scott. Months in, it is still absolutely unbelievable. I don't know if this ever wears off. That feeling of, "Seriously? Is this actually happening?" The shock of it.

Weirdly though I am quickly able to tell the news and stay completely dry-eyed. People tell me I am so strong,

strong as a rock, amazing. Really? Am I just going numb? Surely I should well up when I talk about it, wouldn't that be more human? I remember a friend's dad describing phonecalls with people when they heard they had had bad news, and how he, the owner of the bad news, would carry the phonecall while the person who had phoned to offer love and support just said awkwardly 'yes' and 'exactly', as they literally could not make the words themselves.

Man of the house: "You're phoning to let us know you are thinking of us, thank you so much,"

Caller: "Yes, we are, we are thinking of you so much after we heard the news..." peters out. Pause.

Man of the house: "It's so good of you. If we need anything we will certainly let you know and be in touch."

Caller: "Yes please, please do, just let us know."

Man of the house: "It's so good of you to think of us, thank you."

Caller: "Really you're so welcome, we are thinking of you."

And they hang up and you know a tiny part of them feels slightly relieved to get off the phone. The love is there, we humans just don't always know how to get it out.

CHAPTER 10

Joshie had always had the most beautiful hair. Everyone thinks their child has beautiful hair, and they are right, there are few things better than sniffing your child's clean, soft hair and marvelling that it grows out of their little head – how does it do that? Why does it decide to go in that direction, or to stick up there? Why is it that colour, why is his brother's a different colour? Joshie's was absolutely poker straight, not a hint of a kink to it, and as a toddler it was stripy – all shades of blonde and honey and caramel... Strangers would stop us in the supermarket to say that they would pay hundreds of dollars for highlights like his. Chinese ladies in the shopping mall lifts in Chatswood would admire his haircut and how smoothly it lay against his head (I cut it short at the back but I just couldn't bear to cut into the front, which meant his forehead and eyebrows had never seen daylight. I once attempted a shorter haircut but poker-straight hair is incredibly unforgiving for a mum with haircutting scissors from the pharmacy, unlike Ollie's wavy mop which I could just snip into at the start of each term). And this beautiful hair was about to fall out.

I feel so vacuous, so pathetically vain and materialistic asking the oncology god in one of those shell-shocked early conversations, "Will his hair fall out?" I loathe myself for asking it; in the greater scheme of 'will he live' surely this is a ridiculous thing to ask. But I need to know, it feels like confirmation that this is genuinely leukaemia, not just 'leukaemia-lite' or 'a touch of cancer'. He answers me straight, "Yes, it will, and when it does, it falls out quite fast, probably over one or two days." I say something ruefully about his thick, dark eyelashes and he counters with, "Not all children lose their eyelashes and eyebrows." Something to hope for. I still take close-ups on my iphone that night after he falls asleep of his thick, shiny black lashes against his rosy cheek.

I struggle to get my head around the hair loss thing. This child who had had remarkable hair, whose forehead was white as snow, is it really all going to fall out? What on earth would he look like with a bald head? What if he turned out to have a dent in his skull, or a massive mark on the skin, or a pointed head?! Why does it matter anyway, faced with the enormity of life-threatening leukaemia? And then for every thought I have there is the accompanying guilt for indulging the thought, so in this case: he's a boy, imagine if it was a girl with a long, thick plait of shiny hair, and brushing it or untangling it is a much-loved ritual each day. And all the time, whenever you raise this with any of the medical people the response is the same: it will grow back. Delivered with a smile and a reassuring nod. Never dismissive, but with the weight of experience: they know, they don't verbalise it but they know this is not the worst part of a child having leukaemia. And they also know that really quite a high proportion of the kids don't care at all – apparently they find it weird and annoying at first and then just get on with having no hair.

And so it falls out. They can tell you almost to the day

when it will fall out, so we approach it head on, in stages. I can't bear the thought of going from lovely floppy, shiny, stripy bowl haircut to bald head in one brutal swoop, so we decide to stagger it. One short haircut, and then just before it falls out a really short one with the trimmers. I tell myself this will help Joshie adjust to his forehead but in reality he doesn't seem that bothered, it's all for me. Scott is sad but matter-of-fact. We prepare Ollie and talk to him about saying how cool Josh looks when he has shorter hair, and then no hair. All the time a voice in my head is narrating: 'How appalling is this, having to have this conversation with your seven year old?' Shut up, let me get on with coping. We go for the first shorter haircut at a proper hairdressers. We talk through our strategy with her and realize sadly that hairdressers are experts in cancer hair. Then ten days later, the day before the 'hair loss forecast', we go back for a really short buzz with the trimmers.

By this point the steroids have really kicked in, and my lithe, long-limbed boy is, as mentioned previously, a walking chicken nugget. His little tummy is stretched like a great big balloon, his cheeks, eyes and basically his whole head are puffy, but his 'central fluid retention' means his limbs are still slim. He stands in front of the mirror at bedtime and asks when his tummy will go back to normal. Now, with his brutal haircut, he looks nothing like our child. In fact, he is actually unrecognizable. I scroll back through my phone and stare at photos of him from only four weeks previously, big sparkly brown eyes and rosy gentle cheekbones under a floppy mouse-coloured shock of hair… It is just so hard to find that little person under the big, bloated white moonface, the nearly-bald head and then the grossly enlarged nugget-body. My little man…

As he will be sitting in the hairdressers for his buzzcut for possibly more than twenty minutes, I know he will be ravenously steroid-hungry so buy him a big strawberry milkshake just before we walk in. So he sits there in front of the mirror wrapped up in the hairdressing cloak clutching his milkshake, slurping it down urgently with a prednisone-induced one-track mind, and I want to say to everyone who glances our way, "He has leukaemia, he's on steroids, I'm not an irresponsible mother feeding my overweight kid a giant milkshake, don't judge me…" I feel hollow, almost faint with the exertion of not crying while he is being turned into someone I don't recognize, while I stand by wanting to tell everyone in the hairdressers everything, and also nothing.

Day 29

By now we are travelling up and down to the outpatient oncology clinic at the hospital for chemo every couple of days. The onslaught is well underway. And now that he looks so different and so strange in our home setting I start to feel a perverse relief at being at the clinic. When you walk into that clinic you're just one of many people in the same boat. None of the kids has hair, no-one looks at you and thinks, "Oh my god, that poor family," plenty of the children are puffed up and grumpy and ravenously hungry. Usually it's pretty subdued, but I see one little boy repeatedly thumping his dad, another shouting how much he hates his mum… No-one bats an eyelid, the parents are stoic, calm and firm-voiced; you can almost feel the word hanging in the air: STEROIDS. All the parents look slightly slumped, resigned, weary. And we are in the same boat, however different we may appear to the rest of the world. We, the cancer parents, we are mostly mums, some grannies, the odd dad, we are tall, short, fat, thin, Caucasian, Polynesian, Lebanese, Aboriginal, Asian, headscarves, hotpants, sleek hair, dreadlocks… we are humans.

THE GRATITUDE CLOAK

A few of the parents seem to crackle visibly at t
with impatience and frustration. I make a mental n
one of our first visits not to become impatient. In tact
impatience is an alien concept to me at this point, I seem
to exist in a permanent state of wide-eyed, rabbit-in-the-
headlights gratitude that they are Saving His Life.

For us, for Josh, one of the things that really strikes me
right from the moment we set foot on the oncology ward
is that they know what to do, there is a clearly-defined set
of protocols which he will follow, no-one is feeling around
for answers. This is massive, I can't underestimate how
reassuring it is, despite the fact that no-one can tell us
categorically that he will be fine. It must be a whole
different ballgame if your child has something that stumps
the oncology gods. Over time I become aware of how
incredibly lucky we are that he has Pre-B Cell Acute
Lymphoblastic Leukaemia. A few friends send messages
suggesting we ask the doctors to consider treating him
with various drugs. Whilst their intention is so kind and I
am touched that they have taken the time to look into it,
the idea is so absurd that I have no idea how to respond.
How could I sit there in front of these people who have
decades of knowledge and experience, who sit on global
neuro-oncology boards, have observed countless
international studies, and ask if they would consider trying
xyz? I mean maybe there are parents who do that, but I
would be absolutely writhing in discomfort – I know a bit
about ancient literature, organic food production and
classical music; they know all about paediatric oncology
(the relative irrelevance of my areas of knowledge is not
lost on me either, one way to feel small: meet some
oncologists!). And to be suggesting what they do and kind
of attempting to 'join their medical team' is impossible;
how could I possibly learn their language, absorb
everything they know in a matter of days and speak on the
same level as them? They are the experts, this is

emphatically not my comfort zone, and scrabbling to learn everything about Acute Lymphoblastic Leukaemia whilst also coming to terms with the simple fact that He Has It will finish me off.

We are being fed precisely the right amount of information, exactly what we need to know and no less, no more. I am given the freedom to find that balance for myself, how much I want to know and understand. And they can 'read' me, us as a family. Not only do they know what they are doing medically, but this is a finely-tuned machine and they know exactly what to say to us, what support to offer, how much information to arm us with in order for us to fight our battle effectively, and, crucially, to fight that battle without crumbling into the dust and having a breakdown.

So yes, I would no sooner start suggesting which drugs they use to cure him than ask them to translate the front page of today's newspaper into Latin. (Although part of me reckons they probably could, some of them are that cerebral.)

This makes me think of a conversation Scott had with our oncology god in that first week when Josh was diagnosed. The oncology god was explaining something technical to Scott about cells and chromosomes, and Scott asked him to clarify something, "because I am afraid this is not my area of expertise."

The oncology god smiled beneficently at Scott (he is one of those wonderful, well-groomed, crisp older men who always looks ready for action, with a smile constantly lurking around the corners of his eyes, this is a man who is utterly immersed in such a challenging, potentially tragic field, and yet there is a lightness to him, an energy which I find completely reassuring: this man Knows His Stuff) and with great respect and genuine interest he asked Scott,

"And what is your area of expertise?"

Scott told me he had never felt so small, so like an insignificant gnat on a flea on a mouse. My usually-confident husband mumbled something at high speed about marketing and skyscrapers and developers, and turned the conversation back to leukaemia as swiftly as he could. Slams your own lifepath into perspective.

I remember reading an interview with a woman who had decided to become a barrister as a second career, and she was wavering about whether to go right back and retrain in law.

She said to her teenage son, "The trouble is if I start training now I'll be a barrister at fifty..." to which her son bluntly, and quite rightly, replied, "And if you don't start training now then you won't be a barrister at fifty!"

Maybe there is a medical professional somewhere in one of us yet.

One thing that happens completely organically is that I decide right at the outset that I trust our medical team. I find this an easy decision; I have immense respect for the years and years of education and training that these people have undertaken in order to do something which is ultimately kind: help sick kids. And being slightly obsessed with kindness (our boys, if asked what the most important thing in life is, roll their eyes indulgently and chant, "Kindness and lo-ove...") this gives me a starting point of assuming everyone we encounter is awesome. Later on this becomes more of a mental habit – any time an evil little voice in my head begins with an insidious, "What if someone accidentally connects the wrong..." I have to shut it down, actively, silence it. This whole experience is an opportunity to go certifiably mad with worry, properly mental-asylum-insane. Well I choose not to. If I start suffering from extreme anxiety and madness then all five of us will suffer, so I can't indulge the evil little voice. I get into the habit of telling it to shut up and bugger off. (I like swearing at it.)

We get used to the routine at the outpatient chemo appointments: arrive, sign some stuff, wait among the fellow cancer humans, have bloods taken (thanks to the awesome central line this takes about one and a half minutes and is completely stress-free), choose a cool sticker, wait about forty minutes for blood results, see a doctor to discuss blood results and confirm what's happening today, wait a bit longer and then go through to the chemo 'lounge' (snort – that's my word, it isn't marketed as such thankfully), get connected, hum the opening bars of Stereo MC's Connected (I kid you not, Josh nodding and mumble-singing, 'Gonna get myself, gonna get myself, gonna get myself connected...') and start the day's treatment. And it sounds so ridiculous to say this, but it is, in some ways, a really jolly place.

Chemo nurses are a whole new level of amazing. Some of them are possibly slightly insane in a good way – there is singing, dancing, gobbledegook language, shouts of, "I love you!" at children as they shuffle past. They are incredible, somehow managing to blend such deep, genuine warmth and affection with a no-nonsense practicality and extreme efficiency in a way I have never witnessed in any other setting. They inspire me as a mum; if I can draw on even the tiniest bit of their amazingness with my own children then I will have done a good job. I don't know if any of them realize it but I cling on to them emotionally, memorizing their names as best I can (why do almost all of them start with a D for god's sake? Denise, Debbie, Deb, Diane, Dee... all 24 carat gold, and actually gold enough that I am fairly certain if I used any of the D names they wouldn't mind at all), they are bright beacons in my bleak desert of worry. They unknowingly pass me the Baton of Strength – by modeling joy and amusement and light-heartedness around my child, from Day 1, they show me that he will laugh back, he will live right there and then in that precise moment, and that will make that moment ok. And all you can do is string together lots of moments like that, and suddenly a minute has gone by, and then ten minutes, and then before you know it you have managed to get through half an hour without feeling sombre. These nurses know it and teach it without even realizing they are teaching us.

A side note on feeling sombre: I remember when I was nineteen being dumped by my first love. To be fair I had dumped him the previous year and then realized my mistake and we had got back together, and then ten months after that it was his turn and he dumped me. All for excellent and very normal nineteen-year-old reasons, but I felt like my heart was broken in two. I was in my second year at university, and we 'lived out', which in the spectacularly privileged world of Cambridge meant that you lived outside the walls of your particular college, on an Actual Street in the Town of Cambridge, but the building was still owned and operated by the college, with cleaners and stuff, so it was still light-years away from the real world. Our neighbours up and down the whole street were all students at the same college. Anyway, being dumped meant a lot of time spent gazing vapidly out of my bedroom window onto the pretty street below, and it also meant mind-numbingly endless cups of tea with my friends, looking woeful and glum and analyzing and rehashing and oh god after six weeks I woke up one day and lay in bed staring at the ceiling and thought, 'God this is so boring.' So I got up, got dressed, went to a garden party that afternoon and drank a load of champagne, ate strawberries, again in the privileged world of Cambridge, and met someone else.

So I reckon I can feel down for about six weeks maximum before I get bored. Once the intense, early, crushing days of life-paralysing but necessary and healthy wallowing are over, I find that for me it takes a lot of energy to feel consistently low, I feel heavy and constrained and tied down by it. I start to feel like it's more effort to stay in that state than to go back to living light. And, just to be really clear, I am absolutely not talking about clinical depression here, I consider myself terrifically lucky that I haven't felt myself being pulled towards that devastating black fog. I know people who do have that experience, some close to me, and I see it and my heart goes out to it, I feel intense gratitude that it hasn't beckoned to me so far.

One friend tried really hard to persuade me to take anti-depressants after Scott's spinal cord injury, and although the drama of the idea was quite appealing in a sort of thespian way, I never got round to looking into it and then life just continued and I forgot. Maybe I'm blissfully ignorant of how much better life could be if I did. I don't mean to sound in any way blasé or self-congratulatory about it – in a perverse way it bothered me for a while that I wasn't walking around crying about Josh's diagnosis, why was that, am I missing some emotional gene? No, I think you just get a crash course in 'time and place' and when you still have to brave the school gates, and make packed lunches, and rock a baby to sleep, you just cannot collapse on the sofa and weep at any time. I save it for the darkness of night once they are all asleep. And then the tears come and the damned pillow is wet and the sadness is mixed with indignant anger. And then the storm passes and I feel lighter for having let it come, I experience it and can keep walking until the next storm. The storms aren't nice, but they're also not totally debilitating, they are part of the journey. Hell they are part of being alive! They are honest, and they add colour and richness. Life's rich tapestry. The sunshine feels even warmer and brighter when you've been sitting under a dark cloud.

Anyway, the first love went on to marry a marriage counselor and we are still digital friends. I don't think I ever told him how bored I got of drinking tea and moaning, I feel he would probably approve.

And so to Josh's first chemo appointment. This is daunting, a sort of grotesque parody of a baptism into a world no one wants to be a part of. In the chemo room I encounter the most bizarre dichotomy: fluorescent-coloured bags of horrifically toxic chemicals drip slowly into your child's pristine, hitherto-untouched body while you are surrounded by toys, books, a cheery art and craft table, a big flatscreen and a whole wall of DVDs – we spend the first chemo session colouring in dinosaurs and rocking out to Sing in our reclining armchairs. This is not what I thought chemo would be like. I glance sidelong at him every couple of minutes to see if he looks different, is different, is about to throw up. He is normal. Having said that, the fear of what is to come as all the chemicals accumulate in Josh's body is beginning to gnaw away at me. A couple of armchairs along a teenage boy is slumped in a fetal position on a fully-reclined armchair, Bose noise-cancelling headphones firmly over his ears, eyemask on, wrapped in a white hospital blanket with a hoodie zipped right up to his nose. Under his hoodie he is bald, ghastly pale and clearly wants to shut out the world. His nurse talks to his mum, he is willfully incommunicado. His massive teenage-boy feet in fresh kicks dangle off the end of the footrest. This guy should be out with his mates doing the things that teenagers do, not lying in the bloody oncology clinic. This is just so wrong, this is so, so wrong.

On the menu for this first appointment is a double

whammy of two drugs, one of which says in the notes I am handed, in capital letters, 'IV: FATAL IF GIVEN BY ANY OTHER MEANS.' Right. It also makes his wee fluorescent pink. Today's chemo drugs' medical names (which are long and rather horrifyingly beautiful to pronounce) are shortened to 'vinc' and 'dauno'. I tell this to Scott and we joke that they sound like a retired couple who are off to a dance in the local community hall:

"Awright Vinc? You ready luv?"

"Yeah, coming Daun-o, aww don't you look LOVELY you gaw-juss thing…" kiss kiss kiss.

Vinc 'n' Daun-o. Off to the dance. Dancing around my child's veins, stamping on leukaemia's toes, kicking Luke out of the community hall…. I start to think I am probably going mad. When you're sitting next to your child and this is happening you kind of have to go a bit mad to cope.

And so off we go: a one hour chemo on Tuesday, a three hour one on Friday, a bone marrow aspirate and chemo shot into his spine (both under general anaesthetic) on Monday morning, back to Vinc 'n' Dauno again on Tuesday, a six hour one a few days later, one that sounds like 'asparagus', all interspersed with blood transfusions if and when his haemoglobin gets too low… I remember how we were told that anything that comes out of his body within seven days of chemo is cytotoxic, but clearly as the doses are two or three days apart we will never have the luxury of a seven day stretch without another dose of chemo, so we basically have a cytotoxic son for the foreseeable future. This first protocol goes for about six weeks, then we will have a different but equally intensive cocktail and schedule for the next protocol, then we will start 'Protocol M' (always, always said in a Judi-Dench-in-James-Bond-movie voice), and then another really rough protocol with steroids again all while he has the central line, and then once that is all done he will have oral chemo and regular hospital trips every couple of weeks for a couple of years. All being well. AND THEN WE WILL RING THE BELL.

CHAPTER 11

Oh the bell.

At the outpatient oncology clinic there is an old ship's brass bell, polished beautifully and mounted on a column in the main lobby area. Underneath it is a plaque with the following poem engraved on it:

Ring the bell
With all your might
Ring the bell
Remember your fight
Ring the bell
Ring your fears away
Ring the bell
Celebrate today

The children get to ring it when they finish treatment and are pronounced all clear. We saw a little boy ring it at one of our first visits, the nurses were shouting, "Louder, go on, louder!" and this harsh, clanging, painfully bright sound pierces everything, and everyone - admin, nurses, doctors, men, women, parents, strangers - claps and breaks into cheers, and you kind of collapse with emotion. I can hardly even type that! It is amazing. And as Donna who runs the clinic said to me forcefully, jabbing her finger at me with unashamed ferocity, THAT is the day we are looking towards, that is the day.

Another absolutely gorgeous support device is Josh's string of beads. For every single step of Joshie's treatment (e.g. chemo block, general anaesthetic, bone marrow aspirate, blood transfusion, starting steroids etc) he gets a specific bead to add to his string. The beads are all bright coloured, some are made from glass, some are ceramic, some are clay, and they mark his experience and form a record of what he has had done. So the start of Joshie's string of beads begins with his name 'JOSH' spelt out in cube beads, followed by a silver spike for his cannula going in at the local hospital, then a red flower for his hospital admission, then a little white ceramic dove with outspread wings for his lumbar puncture, a decorative silver stub for the bone marrow aspirate, a blue bubbly glass rectangle for his central line being put in... and so it goes on. My favourites include a little ceramic intricately-painted puffy face to mark the steroid protocols, and eighteen twinkly, faceted crystals in a row for fingerprick tests when he developed steroid-induced diabetes for a while (just to add another educational opportunity for us all) and then the many little white doves – fourteen in total by the end of the string - for his lumbar punctures. Beautiful they may be, but I get a lump in my throat when I remember that the collective noun for doves is a 'pitying'. Yes, he definitely has enough for a pitying of doves.

The beads are a lovely way for Josh to 'own' and accept his experience, and to feel proud of how brave he is, and it is frankly awesome for me to have something aesthetically pleasing to mark each step. They travel everywhere with us in a little cotton pouch, and they dangle from his chemo pole during admissions. We strategically hang the ever-growing string in the window when we stay at my inlaws' house so that a sunbeam hits the eighteen crystals, sending a million tiny dancing rainbows into every nook and cranny of their sitting room. The collateral beauty.

As our journey lurches onwards, both Scott and I see psychotherapists to help us cope and to keep us married frankly. We are told bluntly by the medical team at the start that many, many marriages end in separation and divorce when a child is diagnosed with cancer, the percentage statistic they give us is shockingly high, far, far above 50%. Smugly we think oh that will not be us. Hahahahaha yells the universe, enjoy the ride! So we seek help and accept it and work work work. Our personal beings unravel, separately but still together, with varying consequences (err, still together), but this writing is not about that particular story. However, one day Scott comes home from one of his psych appointments with the news that the leukaemia beads 'have to be buried in a box at some point'. The psych, it turned out, had listened to Scott explaining the concept of the beads, acknowledged their value in the moment, but then suggested that if Josh later developed PTSD or mental health issues relating to the trauma he had been through, then these beads were 'a psychologist's worst nightmare'. We live our trauma, we process our trauma, but then the time comes to say goodbye to our trauma, and not to keep reliving it. We acknowledge that it is part of our story, but we don't need to carry that weight with us. And so we leave it behind. The beads are destined to be put away one day in the future, albeit reverently, in a box. Yesterday is heavy, put it down.

*   *   *

The whole lumbar puncture thing is quite surreal. A

lumbar puncture is when a needle is put into the lower back directly into the spinal fluid that sits around the brain and spinal cord. A sample of the cerebrospinal fluid is taken out and studied so that conditions or illnesses can be diagnosed, but as well as taking fluid out, chemotherapy can also be injected directly into the spinal fluid (called 'intrathecal' chemotherapy). Similarly, a bone marrow aspirate is when a needle is used to go right inside the bone, again usually in the lower back, and take out a sample of bone marrow to test it. Whenever I tell friends or family that he has to have a lumbar puncture or bone marrow aspirate they wince and pull a pained face, and I can't figure out why for the first couple of weeks. Finally, as I gradually emerge out of the fog of shock, it dawns on me that they are assuming it's done awake, as it often is for an adult. Yes, that would be grim. But it's done under general anaesthetic for children, as an outpatient in the clinic – they don't need to be admitted or monitored overnight or anything if it's a regular one. I quickly come to realize that children really are insanely resilient. And also that the clinic has this down to a fine art; it's a production line, like churning out sausages. One child wanders into the operating room, admires the fishtank, hops up on the bed, has a little chat, the team connect the anaesthetic (which again looks exactly like toothpaste in a giant syringe) to his central line, falls gently asleep, the team do their stuff, twenty minutes later the child is wheeled across the corridor into recovery with a tiny band-aid on their back, a new bed is wheeled in, a new child hops up on the bed, their central line is connected… and so it goes on. They do six each morning on 'GA days'.

From my point of view, as the parent, I find it relatively easy to stay relaxed about these GAs once I see how slick and efficient the system is, and how relaxed Josh is. His only complaint as time goes by is that he gets a horrible metallic taste in his mouth each time just before he falls asleep. The minute he is under the team clicks into calm action and they dismiss me with a polite but forceful, "Thank you Mum!" I just have time to dump my Redkite bag in the recovery room, speed-walk to the hospital Starbucks, wait in line, grab my oat milk chai latte (yes, oat milk, Gen X cliché, I'm ok with that, perspective perspective), speed walk back to the recovery room, take a few sips and, "Josh's mum? Here he is just waking up beautifully... all went well..."

They don't always wake up beautifully. Sometimes they wake up and go mental. You learn what your child needs to bring them from anaesthetic fog back to functional small person – fellow oncology mums tell me to try frozen squeezy babyfood pouches to help them wake up more quickly, hot chips to get carbs in them to absorb all the meds... Josh goes through a slightly anti-social phase of insisting on fried calamari rings from the hospital café, which makes the recovery room smell awful and results in me apologizing to everyone, and then thankfully he settles for cheap, mouth-stripping salt and vinegar crisps to combat the metallic taste of the anaesthetic and wake him up inside his head with the loud crunching. The standard request is three bags. I open the first bag for him, and it is like watching a small, drunk person, crisps end up all over the hospital bed and blanket, down his neck, as he shovels them in haphazardly, utterly mal-coordinated and half asleep yet ravenous after fasting pre-GA since the night before. By the second bag he is a little more coordinated, generally half the crisps are eaten and half are sprinkled around or dropped off the sides of the bed on the floor, and by the third bag my boy is back, chatting away contentedly and happy to share the odd crisp with me. Again I marvel at the peculiar twists and turns of life; salt and vinegar crisps were my snack of choice to fend off waves of morning sickness while I was pregnant with each of the boys, the stronger the better, and the taste slams me straight back to happier, if queasier, times. I smile wryly inside as I find the common thread linking both life moments: hope. I was hopeful while pregnant that all would be well, and now hope is becoming more than a thought but an actual course of action for me. Salt and vinegar crisps: the Snack of Hope.

The crisps also serve a secondary purpose of distracting Josh from his life's mission when he wakes up, which is to GET DOWN OFF THE BED. Until we discovered the crisp-distraction, this would involve about ten intense minutes, feeling more like two hours, of me using all my strength to prevent him from launching off the bed and going splat on the floor with his still-sleepy legs. Like a newborn foal. Pretty quickly though the recovery nurses realize how determined he is and we are allowed to relocate to a less public area. I think that's his reasoning, in his anaesthetic fog, he doesn't like being somewhere with loads of people fussing around him and just wants to be normal again. Kind of like the sad, quiet, overall wish: just to be normal again.

During the steroid protocol, when the meds make him constantly hungry and moody, the fasting from the night before the anaesthetic is rough. I learn to do a lot of what is known in hospital-social-worker circles as 'tuning in'. So he says, "I WANT BREAKFAST!" and I reply, "I can hear what you are saying, I understand, you want breakfast."

"BUT I WANT BREAKFAST NOW!"

"I understand that you want breakfast now and you are cross, I understand."

"NO! I WANT FOOD NOW!!"

"I can hear what you are saying, you can have breakfast soon, I understand…"

And so it goes on, god I must be annoying! I would go mental if I was arguing with an adult who kept doing that.

Talk about tuning into what you want to respond to and frankly tuning out what you can't help with, ha! Maybe a good boardroom negotiating tactic.

Another Josh-ism which pretty much all the hospital staff get on board with is the fact, which he states every time he meets his anaesthetist (a different person each time), that, "I actually don't sleep during the day." They look slightly perplexed whenever he announces this as they are connecting the white toothpaste stuff to his lines, and he continues, "I just have a break in the day." We all have to avoid using the word 'sleep' and refer to it as a 'break'. This starts out as a semi-joke but soon becomes part of our regular language, along with words that a five year old should not know like 'methotrexate', 'lumbar puncture' and 'oncology'. Whilst I don't actively shield him from using the real words, he is immersed enough in this new world just to absorb them as part of conversation, and I decide to see it as a positive sign that he is accepting of his current reality. His mental health, at such a young age, appears to be bobbing along ok given the potential for trauma at this point. Acceptance will hopefully help him reach a point of peace when this is a memory. All being well, all being well, whispers the little ever-present voice in my head.

The aftermath of the GAs and lumbar puncture procedures is, to me, nothing short of astonishing. When I think in advance of the whole thing, I realize I am braced for teary kisses as he goes under, nail-biting and pacing during the procedure, hushed loving reassurance in recovery, and at least twenty-four hours of bedside nursing by mummy before he starts to feel like himself again. But no: within an hour he is pretty much back to normal, within two he is firing on all cylinders. He never complains of any discomfort in his lower back, and in fact it isn't until the third one when he is amazed to find a

Kung Fu Panda band-aid floating in his bathwater the next day that he asks me what they actually do during his break in the day. I tell him pretty straight – they inject a shot of your chemo straight into your spine, and they sometimes also take out a bit of bone marrow to see if your leukaemia is gone yet. He nods and says, "Yep that makes sense." There is something so beautiful and calming about the way a 5 year old accepts what he is told and doesn't ask for more. Yes, they are resilient, physically and mentally.

THE GRATITUDE CLOAK

CHAPTER 12

By the time we are a couple of weeks into the first protocol my child now looks and behaves like a different person. Everyone promises me he will go back to normal, physically and emotionally. And three times a day we have to take these damned disgusting life-saving steroids. The stress and drama of this is nothing short of horrific. At home, I crush several tablets each time, mix them with vanilla ice cream and have to follow up with the chaser of the moment, which has to be unwrapped and ready to go the second he swallows the ruined vanilla ice cream. Getting the chaser in before he vomits the steroids up is a fine line. He doesn't vomit them up often, but they are heinous enough that on one or two occasions even the sight of me approaching with a spoon and a regretful face makes him dive across the floor for a sick bag. And with these kind of vital meds, if he vomits straight after taking them you are back to square one as he has to take them again. It is not fun.

I try everything. Explaining why he has to take them (within reason). Being calm but firm. Getting angry. Being funny. Shameful, outright, materialistic bribes. You know that Lego set you really, really want? You can have it if you take them, it's that simple. I don't even have the energy to lace it in age-appropriate, good-parenting language, it's just straightforward bribery. Threatening to get someone else to give them to him. At one point I laughingly wonder in my own head whether parents of older kids offer to pay them. I hear my voice, wheedling, cajoling, and I sound pathetic. I wonder how I am psychologically scarring him trying all these different methods, before seamlessly moving onto the next tactic.

Josh has inherited a staggeringly stubborn streak from Scott. He is furious, flames burning behind his eyes at the outrage of it, shouts at me, does circuits around the house to get away from me... Almost always it ends with me crying in furious exasperation. I'd say on average it takes forty minutes from, 'right Josh,' to, 'f*ck that was hideous.'

The moment now carved into my life's path as 'Peak Hell' arrives midway through this first protocol, we are home and I am trying to get him to take the steroids. Everyone is trying to help without getting in the way, which isn't helpful. After twenty-five minutes of me trying every tactic, he pushes the spoon and little bowl away from him and it splats on the kitchen floor. I have reached the end. I grab my keys, walk out of the house, and get into the car. Tearful wails of, "Mum! MUM!" follow me. Another child, not sure which one, also starts wailing. My mum is with them all in the kitchen, I'm not actually leaving small children on their own, they are safe. I get into the car, shaking and beyond furious, beyond upset, I am a volcano of rage, rage at the unfairness of this, pure rage at the meanness, the cruelty of putting Josh through this, at his stubbornness towards me, at his hatred of me for insisting he take the goddamn medicine. Rage at my being put in this position, rage that there is no one and nothing I can blame, indirect rage, aimless hopeless rage. I start the engine, check the doors and windows are all shut and put it in gear. What on earth do I think I am doing? I have never been so angry and volcanic in my entire life, I'm not about to drive anywhere in this state. I pull forward and drive a little way down the driveway into a clearing surrounded by tall, old casuarina pines. And then I hold my hands firmly on the steering wheel, take a deep breath and I scream.

I absolutely let rip.

"FUUUUUUUCCCCKKKKKKK!
FFUUUUUCCCKKKK!!! AAARRGGHH!!!"

Long, as loud as I can, screaming from the depths of my stomach, absolutely shredding my vocal cords. I used to sing, I was a choral scholar at university, and I know this is the sort of screaming that is wrecking my voice. James Hetfield will approve, I will be able to sing-scrape Enter Sandman very well. In fact Metallica might not be heavy enough, this is more a moment for that (to me) incomprehensibly livid death metal. Maybe their kids had cancer. I stare at the pine trees through the sunroof, gasping for breath, I stare at my hands on the wheel, a thousand question-words tumble through my panicked brain – What? Where? What? I cannot...I CANNOT!! How? HOW???

This is my breakdown.

Luckily the Volvo XC70 has double glazing as well as compressed airbags in every possible nook and cranny, because it is Swedish and Safe, which means it is about as sound-proofed as one of those rooms with padded walls they have in recording studios. So as far as I know, nobody heard me, although I couldn't give a flying monkey's bum about that at this point. And actually the nearest people, if they were home, are our neighbours, and they have their own cancer experience, so they would get this anyway.

I am destroyed, this has destroyed me. I cannot do this. I don't know how, I don't know how people do this.

I sit there for a few more minutes and then I think, "Right." I don't get some wave of new energy or some epiphany or dawning of strength or anything. I feel completely helpless. Floundering.

And then I park the car back in the carport, get out, go back into the house and continue to try to give Joshie his medicine. I don't know how I did it that time, I look back and I honestly don't remember how we did it each time, three times a day for weeks, and then again during a later treatment protocol. We got through mountains of jelly snakes. I ceased caring about whether bribing your child is morally irresponsible. My perspective on what makes a good parent (ha ha ha ha ha) is forever altered. Context is everything.

When there isn't any choice, you have to keep going, because you can't do anything else.

CHAPTER 13

When we have early starts at the outpatient chemo clinic we stay the nights either side with my inlaws. They immediately get it – wholesome, home-cooked meals, laundry is just done, it's a familiar environment for Josh which is so important when his days are full of strange new adults talking and staring at him. Like the dinner ladies back home, this is the support which enables us to cope. Without it, without grandparent love and calm and cheer, I have no idea what we would do. I was warned early on that the siblings can really suffer when a child is diagnosed with leukaemia; the long, long treatment timeframe – a two year marathon not a six week sprint - and the unpredictability of hospital stays means siblings often have to be picked up by or dropped off with different people, all of whom constitute the 'support team', but are ultimately 'back-up'.

With grandparents on both sides (well, three in action) we manage to avoid this. My mum uproots her UK life to fly around the planet and become Ollie's consistency personified. Flight insurance is activated, immigration is bombarded with letters from the hospital team, she can stay longer-term than normal. She and Ollie develop a uniquely concrete bond which has not wavered as time has passed – it helps that he looks like her and likes to tell everyone he has 'blue eyes like Granny P'. Scott's parents develop a really special relationship with little eleven month old Albie, with gruff but immensely loving Papa taking him along to a local playgroup and Albie crowing gleefully, "Papa! Papa!" whenever we drive up to their house. I can see why one granny I speak to in the waiting room at the clinic says that having a granddaughter with leukaemia had a wonderful effect on the family; everyone comes together if they possibly can because they have to, and because they care, and, well, because of love. She actually says the words, in quiet, halting, Arabic-accented English, "It has been a good thing for my family," and I smile and nod because I am a well-brought up English girl who smiles and nods politely, and think WTF? But now I absolutely see she had a point.

In the throes of steroids and Vinc 'n' Dauno I sometimes dare to leave Josh with the inlaws, fully dosed up with super-strength anti-emetics to stop him feeling nauseous, and armed with a couple of sick bags, and grab an hour or two at the shopping mall on my own to get stuff done (Christmas is looming) and I start to notice completely different things. It's that familiar human thing of seeing whatever is painfully relevant to your life at that time. So when I had a couple of shocking but ultimately uncomplicated first-trimester miscarriages a few years previously, I saw pregnant women everywhere I looked. Everywhere. Extra glow-y ones. Friends going through IVF talk about seeing newborn babies at every turn. And now, for me, it is mums with teenage boys at the shopping mall.

It's the teenage boys who give me such a pang rather than boys who are Joshie's age, the teenagers represent the future I long for, one we had imagined would just happen. I see a mum ahead of me in the queue at the Target checkout with two boys, close in age just like Ollie and Josh would be, maybe thirteen or fourteen ish, with tousled, surfy, sun-blonde hair and long, caramel, skinny limbs. (They are at that age of spots and gangly awkwardness, but this being Australia they somehow manage to look sunny and outdoorsy and healthy with their only-slightly-pimply skin.) Their body language exudes that young teenage agony I remember so well which screams, 'I am out with my MUM but I am WAY too cool for this, how did this HAPPEN if I bump into anyone I know I am going to DIE!' and simultaneously whispers, 'Not quite confident enough to be out on my own doing my thing and besides I need socks and undies and Mum knows what sort I like.' But more than this, it is their interaction with each other which punches me in the stomach. They are right in each others' personal space with heads tilted back and laconic smiles on their faces, legs lolling around and hands flicking at each other, they are absolute craftsmen at knowing how to wind each other up. An ex-boyfriend of mine was one of four brothers, and even though they were all in their twenties, I would watch the fraternal bonds being so precisely twanged and teased and heckled, the tiny nuances in physical movements or expressions which they knew would make one of the others incandescent with rage... they had mastered the art, over years of practice, of ripping the shit out of each other. And so these two at the checkout, you could feel the brother-bond crackling off them like static, keeping it just in check as they were in a public space and the checkout girl's eyelashes were fluttering...

Please, please, pleeeeease let Ollie and Josh be like that. Please. Let him make it through this hideous time, let him come out strong and completely cured. Let him be one of the good statistics, not one of the exceptions.

Every cell in me begs and pleads. Let him have floppy carefree hair that teachers purse their lips at on Speech Day, let him feel the surf sucking at the sand under his feet, let him lust after girls (or boys – it really doesn't matter), just let him be healthy and keep living, please… I don't know who I am imploring this speech to. I am not one for clasping my hands in formalized prayer, walking among the paediatric oncology ward and believing this was all god's plan is not an option for me personally. But to me there is something greater, whether we call it god or another word, whatever we perceive god to be, I still send out this deeply spiritual yearning into the wind, into the trees, into Mother Nature, into the ether, the universe… It's a wish. Josh gets every blown-out candle wish, every one of my eyelash wishes right from the moment he is diagnosed. 'Let Josh get better, for good. Whoosh…'.

Day 36

Somehow we come through the Protocol 1A and launch straight into the next. This one has different chemo drugs which are given half at the main hospital in Sydney, and half at our local hospital, so we bounce around from nurse team to nurse team and start feeling like we really know everyone. We have got this, Josh. I begin to see newly diagnosed children in the waiting room at the clinic, children with beautiful glossy hair and wide-eyed, shell-shocked parents. One stunningly supermodel-esque, fine-boned mum in an Arabic abaya and sheyla asks me a question (in a broad Aussie accent), it turns out her daughter has the same diagnosis as Joshie, and is one of 3 girls. And this voice comes out of me which absolutely startles me: I am smilingly telling her how to pick up her daughter's meds from the hospital pharmacy, giving her tips on how to avoid the long, long waiting times, and then pointing her towards the best hot chips for after a general anaesthetic… What has happened? I am confident, friendly. I am talking like I know my stuff. I am reassuring her, I think I even say the words, "I've been there, you're not alone…" This is weird. It crosses my mind that I hope I don't sound annoying, a know-it-all, I certainly don't feel like that, I feel like I'm hugging her, albeit with words. She clings onto every word. I pass on tips from G's mum, the things she told me in that horrendous first week when she showed us G's central line (seal the dangly central line caps in a ziplock bag and micropore tape it to her shoulders during bath time), we end up saying something like 'we are going to get through this' and half-laughing with our mouths while our eyebrows are knotted in anguish.

As we drive home that day I am amazed at myself. I still feel emotionally in shock, in the greater scheme of things, but I appear to have graduated a level. He has no hair, we have a whole treatment protocol, a horrendous protocol at that, under our belts now, I can reel off the names of all his drugs and when and where he takes what – chemo clinic, home, whatever – I know the way the places work. I don't for one moment feel pleased with myself. With this realization of my acceptance and, for want of a better word, newfound capability, comes an even deeper respect and gratitude for our medical team. It is only because of their care, education, manner, approach, the full Monty, it is only because of that that I have been able to graduate to the next level. A shakier, less kind system and I would still be on shaky ground.

We can do this.

That doesn't mean I don't cry. Music is my key to unlock this. As we barrel up and down the highway time after time to and from outpatient clinic appointments, Josh starts requesting his favourite songs and we make a playlist. Top of the list is Insomnia by Faithless. He loves it, goes wild in the back seat, drumming and raving like a chicken-nugget shaped whirling dervish. He demands I turn it up louder and louder, until our ears are completely filled with the sound, no space left for thought, and as the track builds up and up my tears pour down my face, it is so full on, this is so full on. The intensity of everything is so perfectly expressed in a powerful track.

Anyone who knew me from my childhood would probably be amazed that it isn't classical music which is my therapy – as a child I was strong-armed by a Tiger Father into being a 'child prodigy' on the piano, then French horn, and then I escaped to university and pretty much ditched both those in favour of singing. Horn players have good strong lungs, I could make an ok noise. I briefly contemplated training to be a professional singer, but my then-other-half displayed such a deep-rooted, quiet conviction and belief in his own abilities (he was and is a professional singer) that one day I looked at myself and thought, 'I don't have that self-belief. I love singing, I love the round, fat noise and the feeling it gives me inside my body, but I don't like being stared at.' And if you don't like being stared at, being a musician probably isn't the right thing to pursue. Especially singing, where it's just your body, not even an instrument to share the limelight. So I let the singing slide, played the piano a bit just for my own entertainment, sold the horn and gave myself the freedom to enjoy music just for music's sake. In this life phase, one of my favourite genres is music that has been cleverly mashed and reimagined, creatively fused: 1 Giant Leap, the live orchestral version of Insomnia performed at the BBC Proms in London a few years ago… Hence Faithless. Ironically named, given this life phase demands absolute faith.

At this point we have also recently discovered the movie Sing, so the soundtrack features heavily in Josh's car playlist requests. The songs he likes best are almost ridiculous in their aptness. His all-time favourite, which could possibly be because it is sung by a gorilla and Josh likes strong animals, is I'm Still Standing. Again jacked right up, he quickly memorises all the words, and there is something absolutely gut-wrenching about a bald little five year old who is going through the most aggressive chemo regime, sitting in the back seat of your car, bopping around as much as his booster seat will allow him yelling, "I'm still standing! YEAH YEAH YEAH!" I love that he does this, I love how it transports him completely, he sings the words like he really, really means them, I love his innocence at why it would make me cry. And I am of course a total wreck, my hands grip the steering wheel and I sob-laugh with love for this little human being who is so treasured, so loved by us and is having to deal with such horrors. It is so bloody unfair on him.

For I'm Still Standing I also improvise my own seriously awesome (well, awesome to me!) backing vocals over the top, which take the song to the next level. When the tune descends I soar up and over it (trust me, it's good!), and if I'm feeling strong I really go for it, properly wobbling along, full operatic core support engaged, with Joshie and Johnny the gorilla. More often than not though, my voice cracks with emotion when I try to sing, no matter how much breath I take and how I support it; this is beyond me. I remember one other time, far, far worse, trying to sing in the school choir at a dear friend's brother's funeral. Singing when you're torn apart with emotion is really, really hard. Horrible agonized mouse-squeaks come out. It is impossible for me.

And then he loves My Way, sung by a tiny weeny (and quite mean) mouse, but sung very well, and also fairly appropriate lyrics for a little boy fighting a big fight, and then the other proper tear-jerker is the elephant's song,

Don't You Worry About A Thing. This one I decide to take at face value and imagine I am being comforted – don't worry, it's going to be alright.

Through the entire two year span though, the song that wins the medal for consistently breaking mummy is Rachel Platten's Fight Song. Every single line takes on almost-impossible significance, starting with his little voice - he is the small boat on the ocean - building to heart-exploding proclamations about taking back his life, everybody worrying about him, fire in his bones, proving he is alright and he's still got a lot of fight left in him. It makes me crumble even just paraphrasing the lyrics. The song even mentions how it's been two years of missing his home, his normality, matching his overall planned two years of treatment. I feel genuine physical pain inside my chest when we listen to it, part of me desperately wants to turn it off to escape this loss of control, but I can't, I can't, this is a living experience and I know by now that if I can just get through it and sob, crumble, whatever word I want to use for it, then when it finishes I will be fractionally lighter, fractionally stronger in that lightness. Thank you Rachel, whoever and wherever you are in this big wide world.

I always feel slightly self-conscious when ginormous semi-trailers overtake us on the highway (this is Australia – unlike in the UK, enormous lorries are inexplicably allowed to go at the full speed limit, in any lane, and they often seem to take great pride in terrorizing all other vehicles on the road, it's really quite frightening) imagining the 'I'm the king of the road' style truck driver glancing down into our car as he roars past and sees a little bald cancer boy shout-singing and a mum with tears pouring down her face and a very unladylike sobbing grimacing mouth… Even more tragi-comic when you consider that I'm fairly likely to be sobbing to a gorilla, a mouse and an elephant.

The musical drives are probably the time I cry most throughout the whole thing. You have to gather such strength, such a shield to face the normal world, with your child almost constantly by your side, that accessing the tears doesn't come easily to me on a day to day basis. You can't let the shield crack. But for me music is such a massively powerful key to emotion and feeling, it only takes the thought of a track sometimes to make me well up. I always have to check my mascara before getting out of the car, take some deep breaths, gather up all the pieces of myself into a solid whole again. Joshie never seems disturbed or upset by me crying. Ollie would, and Scott would too – he will be livid when he reads this; crying on the Hume Highway is NOT SAFE. True, true. I cried on the bloody Sheikh Zayed Road driving up and down to Dubai and Abu Dhabi too, processing the husband with the spinal cord injury. I am a woman who cries on highways.

CHAPTER 14

So back to this new protocol, and in this one, the dominant chemo, whilst doing its job, can actually also cause fevers as a side effect, so we are warned that regardless of whether he is exposed to some sort of infection or not he may spike to 38 degrees. If this happens, we still have to go straight to Emergency and be admitted, as there is no way of knowing if it's an infection, or 'just' a side effect. And spike he duly does... Luckily we are so well prepared for this by the amazing medical team, and I am such a nerdy organized geek-mum by this point, that both Josh and I feel as though we are acting out a drill we have already learnt. Of course he spikes just as I am on my way to bed doing a late-night temperature check. Our Action Plan directs us to the local hospital if this happens when we are home, which we are, and once we are safely tucked up in our hospital bed / armchair on the paediatric ward, I feel an odd mix of resignation and relief: now we know the system works, and it is all ok. The staff are phenomenal; there is a slight sense of occasion – like us, they have also been briefed by the Sydney hospital on exactly what to do when Josh presents, and how quickly to do it, and leukaemia is not something they have all seen before. A gorgeous nurse even has my armchair bed made up and ready by the time we reach our room, this beautiful care makes me well up, this is going above and beyond. As we settle in for the night, there is an unspoken gentle triumph in the air, we all did what we were meant to and now Josh and I are going to bed for a night of beeping, knowing you angel-nurses are watching over us from your station just outside the door. Thank you, thank you, thank you for your love, your humanity. Sometimes the gratitude almost knocks the breath out of me. I am completely muffled, bundled in my gratitude cloak. I say thank you slightly more than is socially acceptable, I hope they can really feel it.

When Josh is admitted to our local hospital he is always put in an isolation room. Often we are the only people on the children's ward, in a little, peaceful bubble with the magnolia tree nodding outside the window and our favourite café on the street outside less than a minute's walk from Josh's room. The wonderful nurses are local and know our daily life. But when we stay in the main children's hospital in Sydney, back at the mothership, the busy oncology ward is a place where a different type of bond is forged. I develop unique friendships with the other parents on the ward, sometimes even wordless friendships. As we pass in the corridor we exchange knackered glances of solidarity which sometimes develop into conversations. Sometimes I don't look at anyone at all because I can't and I know that is understood too. And the thing I knew beforehand but really hadn't appreciated until it was right there in my face, was how completely non-discriminatory cancer is. A fully-niqabbed-up mum smiles (err, with her eyes) at me over the toaster. A New Caledonian family chat and cry in French. Chic Surfer Mum sharing our room for one night wells up with me and we compare our levels of disbelief that this Is Actually Happening and feel the pain together, we land at a very ineloquent point of just shrugging and saying, "It's just shit." It's insane. And we all speak this godawful language of multi-syllabic medication names and numbers... The language of Mordor.

And the more time we spend on the ward the more it dawns on me how lucky we are to have a straightforward diagnosis. Over time we share rooms with children who have solid tumours, brain tumours, extremely rare types of leukaemia... ours is one where studies and trials have been tweaked and meticulously adjusted so that they know what to do. The idea of having the absolute top specialists stumped must be another level of fear entirely. Always the bonding question between the parents is, "How did you find out, how did they discover it?" The stories are objectively fascinating, emotionally gut-wrenching, heart-breaking. Everyone wells up for the other person when they hear it. Having a really good GP seems to be the holy grail – those whose GPs dithered for a few months are in much worse shape than the rest. We are one of the very lucky ones. A lot of the stories involve a completely unrelated accident; a broken arm at Saturday soccer, an x-ray, a reaction of: "Never mind the bone, what's THAT?!" Or a trip to the dentist who noticed a bulge at the back of the mouth, x-rayed the teeth and found a completely hidden tumour filling up the sinus cavity behind the cheekbone. Each story is terrifying and panic-inducing in its own right, and now I see why the advice I was given at the start is so crucial: talk to people, listen to their story, and then let it float away, don't get drawn into it. You are on your own path and they are on theirs. I know the other parents understand this too; it's absolutely ok to share stories and then draw the psychedelic Aussie animal curtains around your cocoon and go back to your own child. Nothing is more important than your own child.

At one of our scheduled admissions there's a child on

the ward having radioactive iodine treatment. This is not the same thing as radiotherapy, which is given externally, so the radiation passes through your body. You can have radiotherapy and then go home. Radioactive iodine therapy, however, is a type of internal radiotherapy, which leaves your body actually radioactive for several days. You can't leave hospital until the radiation in your body has come down to a safe level. This is bonkers, properly mind-blowing for me; here I am with my child having 'regular' high dose chemo on a twenty-four hour drip, followed by rescue drugs to make sure his kidneys are ok, and Josh is having what I am told by the oncology god is a 'boring' experience of it (boring in this situation makes you want to throw a party, this is a Good Thing), and meanwhile on the other side of the corridor people dressed in what look like hazmat suits are taping white sheets over everything. It's like the final scenes in ET. The child's family has flown from overseas as this hospital is one of very few which provide this treatment, and the ward is abuzz with energy and a surprisingly positive excitement. The parents look focused, calm, smiling politely as we pass, completely together. The mum does not look in any way 'wrecked'. My fellow-parent in our room and I agree that we would probably look a bit wrecked, but then it dawns on us that this is possibly something they have been waiting for, planning, almost looking forward to in a momentous way, it is progress. They don't appear shell-shocked or floundering at all. I say this as an observer, inside they may all have been screaming and running for the hills, but they are properly holding it together. Interested doctors from other parts of the hospital crowd around the window peering into the room through the glass, an ICU nurse is at the window twenty-four hours a day. One of our favourite nurses comes into our room with a slightly manic air and announces with a flourish as though she is introducing a performer on Broadway, "I have just made a child radioactive!" We gape nervously, is she OK, is she in shock? Nope, this is all in a day's work for her. Plus she's a true professional, she knows we parents must all be furrowing our brows and worrying about what is going on, she knows how to diffuse us.

I fall a little bit in love with this same nurse when she tells me her night shift strategy. On the oncology ward, nurses are often in charge of two patients (or sometimes even just one) for the duration of their shift. Rooms are either isolation rooms for one, or rooms for maximum two children. If this particular nurse is caring for both the children in a shared room, she sets up their drips so that they finish at the same time and then sets herself the challenge of getting back to the drip to sort it out before it starts beeping, thus ensuring the children and parents aren't woken up. Usually if you start beeping you have to press the Nurse button to let them know you need help, which involves being dragged from sleep by the beeps, listening carefully enough to work out if it is you or your neighbor beeping (the machines are often only a metre or so apart, although the psychedelic animals give you privacy), finding the Call button and then pressing it. And each child is probably having several different meds throughout the night and will therefore beep a lot. So her strategy, so caring, so deliciously nerdy and satisfying, is the sort of thing which makes the difference between feeling like crying all of the following day, and being able to cope and smile at everyone the following day. I nearly weep with grateful excitement when she is our night nurse for the first time, and I can confirm that her strategy works. She has angel wings sprouting from her back. With pillar-box red feathers because that is the kind of colour-person she is. They all have angel wings sprouting from their backs. They are incredible humans.

CHAPTER 15

Day 75

I become quite intolerant, in this brutal phase of inflicted perspective. My top three intolerances, seventy-five days into Josh's treatment, are:

1. Coming back from a hospital admission with Joshie and other people saying how tired they are. Tired of just daily life with regular healthy kids who don't have to take medicine throughout the day, who have beautiful hair, who can run and jump without you inhaling sharply and wincing at the risk of bruising or falling and getting an infected graze or or or… it is endless. But balancing this is an instant and loving interest and empathy for anyone going through any medical experience.

2. Parents being stroppy and disrespectful to teachers about things that just don't matter in the greater scheme of things. Umm, is your child at risk of dying? No? I reckon you will probably be ok then. I deal with this intolerance by being as grateful and appreciative to our teachers as I

have the energy for. They know my children in a way I don't; they care, they chose to care and educate children all day every day. Amazing.

3. People being rude about hospitals. As I am someone who does not like drama and confrontation (my husband would dispute this, but I think it is fine for spouses (spice?) to be participants in respectful, healthy confrontation, how else are you meant to live for the rest of your life with a human who has a different brain to your own?), I display my intolerance when people are rude about hospitals with a closed-mouth smile and sympathetic eyes. But it is a tough one, and I don't like how it makes me feel about myself. I don't like feeling cross with people or cross with the world, it ruins your day when something deflating happens.

But although I get into the habit of stomaching these small, ultimately understandable stresses that other non-paediatric-oncology-people have (let's face it I was one of them until recently so I know how it feels), occasionally the rage hovering beneath the surface spills out. Reversing out of my parking spot one day shortly after he was diagnosed, I was shouted at by a harassed-looking woman in a nippy silver car who thought I was about to reverse into her.

"Use your mirrors MUM!!!" she yelled at me, loading the word 'mum' with disparagement and annoyance. I can see her now, angry frown, hair scraped back, massive sunnies hiding half her face.

I take a deep breath, keep the car still, wind down the windows and take a massive breath and at the absolute top of my voice I scream back at her, "JUST SHUT UP!!!!!!" Like, quite high-pitched like a potentially certifiably mad person. Like one of Macbeth's witches maybe. Or a banshee. Yes, I was a screeching banshee.

I see her startle. She stops her car and half of me hopes she gets out and I can let rip about Josh into this poor woman, but I think I might actually have scared her and after a moment she slowly starts driving out of the car park.

Slightly awkwardly I then end up following her same route, both of us driving ridiculously carefully and I-am-so-calm-ly (this is a town of Nice People), and I can see her at each mini roundabout glancing at me in her mirrors. I have an awful, awful feeling I have seen her somewhere before, she's probably a school mum – for one dreadful moment I think she might be one of the teachers from Josh's preschool. Finally to my disproportionate DELIGHT she turns off a different way and we are separated. I spend the next few days looking out for a zippy nippy silver car feeling extra paranoid. I splurge to a dear friend on the phone that evening who reassures me that when I said I'd 'done something awful' she was not expecting something as innocuous as shouting at another car. God I am pathetic.

Anyway I realise some people are tough enough to have altercations like this and just shrug them off, but for me, now, this is properly depressing and deflates my strength for the rest of the day. It demonstrates in an instant how fragile the emotional shield is that is holding me together, and how close to the surface my rage and fury is bubbling. I resolve to get some therapy somewhere along the line.

People being rude about hospitals is a weird one. I just don't get this. A couple of people remark that they think I am amazing and they 'just don't know how you can do it, sitting there day after day in a hospital', they hate hospitals, they say, awful places. Whilst it is nice to be called amazing (I do not feel amazing, I feel like I am scrabbling) I am so uncomfortable with this sentiment - awful places - really? Really? I mean sure, the fluorescent strip lighting isn't relaxing and the ugly medical kit isn't hidden away behind closed doors, and it's bloody annoying if you end up at an urban Emergency Department in the middle of the night for some reason in normal life, afraid and in pain, have a long wait, observe a load of drunk people wasting the doctors' and nurses' time with their self-inflicted miseries and then finally get to see a doctor, but surely, surely at some point you have a basic realization that the people who work here are helping people they have literally never met before. Strangers, essentially.

Joshie was dying when we were admitted, and they stopped him dying. Every second that ticks by when we are inside a hospital is one second closer to him ringing that bell. And we could not do this without them. It's that simple. To paraphrase Hugh Grant in Four Weddings, I am in bewildered awe of hospitals. I know there are some that struggle, of course, I know negligence and inexperience and mistakes happen, I know that and I can only speak for the handful of hospitals we have frequented in Abu Dhabi and Australia, but they feel like massive, humming, sturdy temples of hope, stuffed full of remarkable people doing remarkable jobs every single day. The cleaners in hospitals are really nice. They always smile when they come into your room and then clear up, in some cases literally, poo off the floor. They are part of the fabric of what makes hospitals work. Imagine if there weren't any cleaners. My point being that everyone who works in any capacity in a hospital is helping you. Even the hospital café staff dolloping six-hour-heat-lamp lasagna onto a sterilized plastic tray, they're helping. They're serving us. Coming down off my high horse, I also quite like that the lights are always on twenty-four hours a day, hospitals are never shut. We are always ready to help you. Even the car park attendants who validate our tickets every time we visit may be bored, but they're smiley and cheerful. Maybe it's a children's hospital thing, but Scott's spinal ward in Abu Dhabi was the same. All nationalities of workers, humming together like a giant hive, trying, trying.

Hospitals are places where things happen, things get done, progress is made. When you're in hospital you are on the railroad tracks, on the road to recovery, steaming along. When you're home, it is undeniably blissful to be home (walking into my bedroom after a hospital stay and just looking at our bed with pillows and a duvet and sheets usually makes me well up), but home is where you go between the action. And besides, when we are home I am the one in charge of caring for him, which is pretty daunting. There's a definite relief in arriving at the hospital and knowing that for as long as we are there he is in the care of professionals.

On the wall in the Parents' Room on the ward is a poster with quotes from fellow oncology parents. One of them brings me up short, it reads something along the lines of, 'We live eight hours away from the hospital, and being at home is hard. Family and friends make me feel awful. Being here on the ward is our new home for now.' Family and friends make me feel awful? This poor person, what is happening here? And then it clicks: when you're home you're perceived as sick, 'that family', other people are focused on what is wrong, and so they respond to you accordingly. When you're in the hospital you are one of many people who are in the heady throes of Being Fixed. And staff and other patients respond to you with great positivity; so we've achieved this, next up we're doing this, he's looking great today! How are you mister, that is one cheeky smile!

For me, the person's quote isn't quite true; in my case it is the well-meaning support of family and friends which makes me feel I am not alone. Feeling alone and going through this would be truly hard. And I do feel terrified, daunted, crushed at times by the enormity of what is happening, despite my ability to put on my emotional shield and keep plodding on. Having caring people recognize that and offer kind words sort of validates my own wobbly feelings. But I can see what they mean. Coming to the hospital, and especially the ward, is a relief. A slight lifting of the weight off my shoulders; it's a shared burden, shared with the other parents, even if I don't know the ones we encounter each time. And shared with the staff, the amazing staff who understand.

I have immense respect for hospital employees' feet. Imagine being on your feet all day long. Just that. I did a few food trade shows in my 20s and didn't sit down all day. Nothing stressful - would you like to sample some organic, dairy-free, sucrose-free chocolate? - but absolutely knackering! I was young, fit, skinny after a traumatic break-up, wearing cute, flat, comfy ballet pumps... still had to lie on the hotel bed in the evening with my legs up the wall to get the blood to go away from my feet. That's a hilarious memory, my work colleague and I with our legs up the wall in the Hotel de Costes in Paris no less, giggling about how daft we looked and listening to the early-evening Summer bustle on the street below in the Marais as the bars began to fill up with Chic People. Yes, being on your feet for a day is tiring, then factor in the demands of a hospital ward: running around, doing procedures, making decisions, calculating accurate medicines which cannot be wrong, keeping small children calm, keeping their anxious parents calm (ha!), constantly being 'up' and 'switched on' and in professional mode... AND the emotional toll of actually caring about your patients, not just for them. It beggars belief. So we try to smile at them and be nice as much as we can. And I can report that you do indeed reap what you sow, because we are smiled back at pretty much one hundred per cent of the time.

CHAPTER 16

Day 86

Christmas is hurtling towards us now and I start to feel a slow-rolling, steady wave of guilt washing over me that it is going to be so different this year. How can I try to create the dreamy childhood Christmas the boys are gearing up for with all this going on around us? How can I do all the special things, the decorations, the extra shopping, the sort of food... I can't. Mum and I work out what is essential and what can fall by the wayside, and as we talk it dawns on me that these boys are one, five and seven, they are going to have an awesome Christmas, provided Josh manages to stay out of hospital, regardless of what we do at home, because it is Christmas and their stockings will be filled and there will be a Christmas tree covered in decorations. They really don't care about cranberry sauce and holly. I dig out the Elf soundtrack, Carols from Kings and my Reggae Christmas Remixed album, and we're away: instant Christmas.

But protocols don't pause for festivals and holidays, and our schedule shows 25th December as the festive filling in a sandwich with chunky slices of chemo bread on either side. Our anxiety levels increase as the date gets closer in case he spikes a fever and has to be admitted, I ache in hope that he will wake up on Christmas morning in his own bed. The Greek gods are merciful this time: Christmas is celebrated at home, with itchy tinsel tied around his bald head, oral medication taken between mince pies and turkey roasted beautifully by my mum, and party hats and endless chocolate coins and little boy squabbles. I'd like to say we forget everything for a day, but of course we don't. If anything our context is made even more intense by the giant, unspoken words hanging over us constantly: please let this not be his last Christmas, please let him have many more.

The day after Boxing Day we move on to the 'middle' protocol, Protocol M (in Judi Dench's voice) which involves inpatient hospital stays of a few days alternating with ten days at home. Josh is given high doses of a potent chemo drug over twenty-four hours, and as the first admission approaches I start to worry about this one. The oncology god talks about how it is a particularly challenging protocol as families are divided, geographically split up, childcare for siblings becomes harder to organize... We get our ducks in a row and work out that for each admission we will be spread across three different places: my mum and Ollie at home being normal, Josh and I in hospital, Albie and Scott with his parents nearer to us. Scott and I come up with strategies, tactics, ways we can keep a close eye on Ollie's mental health and feel confident that he isn't becoming anxious. Mum agrees to make these times special for her and Ollie – I tell her that anything goes at these times provided she is comfortable with his requests (and each time I come home to a stunning array of sweets, sugar-laden breakfast cereals and, oddly, a frankly inexplicable number of packets of different-shaped pasta – I counted nine at one point, weird), and each weekend before Team Sydney sets off, Scott and I take Ollie out on our own to tell him how proud we are of him, give him the opportunity to ask any questions or voice any worries, and stuff him full of ice cream.

As well as these little 'trio' outings for Ollie with both of us parents, I also take him out for what becomes known as a 'therapy milkshake' between Joshie's admissions and whenever I get the chance to be just the two of us, and he knows this is his chance to vent. In my mind I have some sort of idyllic maternal vision of this being like a scene from a movie, Ollie with beautiful liquid blue eyes and floppy hair, vulnerable yet calm, snuggling into me in a squishy café armchair as I hug my hot chocolate and hold his gaze with a loving smile on my lips, something like this:

Ollie: "Actually Mummy I am worried about Joshie. I love him so much and I still fight with him when we play Lego, which makes me sad when I lie in bed and he has already fallen asleep. And I worry that he might die."

Me: "Darling I am so proud that you felt you could tell me this. We all love Joshie very much, and you know actually having normal brother-fights with him is a good thing as it means that neither of you is changing who you really are because of his leukaemia. You are still lovely Ollie like you always have been, and he is still lovely Joshie like he always has been."

Ollie: "But what about him dying? Is he going to die?"

Me: "You know Ollie, Josh has the best doctors, and they know how to make him better, and everyone loves him very much. We are very lucky that the doctors know what to do to give him the best chance of being completely cured."

Ollie: "I feel better now. Thank you for the milkshake. I love you Mummy."

Me: "I love you too darling, you are doing so well and Daddy and I are really proud of you. Any time you want to ask me a question, you can."

But what actually happens is this:

Me: "Ollie is there anything you're worried about, do you have any questions you were wanting to ask me? School...Josh...you can talk if you feel like it..."

Ollie, pausing from his noisy slurping: "Nah. So the thing I love about Volvos is the way you can just press the button on the door of the boot and it closes so it's not heavy and you don't have to get your hands dirty."

I. Kid. You. Not.

Right at the start, when we all came home after his initial week in hospital, Ollie did ask us if Joshie was going to die. Scott and I were waiting for it and had planned our response. As stated above, we told him Josh had the best doctors, they knew how to try to make him better and that everybody loved him very much. He accepted it absolutely and ran off to do something else. We have been so lucky with the ages of our boys through this journey. They think of a question, ask it, you can answer it straight without elaborating, and they accept it and move onto the next thing (invariably Lego, Octonauts or David Attenborough at the moment).

One way this is painfully but beautifully demonstrated is when we talk about our dear friend A. Both boys, separately, come to their own realization that Josh has the same thing as A: "Mummy it's the same as A's word: leukaemia."

To each of them, making no allowances for their age difference, I explain that A had something called Acute Myeloid Leukaemia, and Josh has Acute Lymphoblastic Leukaemia. Can they hear there is a different word in the middle? Yes. Well there are lots of different kinds of leukaemia, and very, very sadly lovely A had one which is really hard for the doctors to sort out, and it is also harder to make adults with leukaemia better. The doctors tried and tried, but very sadly she died. I well up, and we hug and talk about A's children and her husband, and how the love she gave them will always be there in their hearts, nothing will ever take that away even though she is gone. And then we move onto how very lucky Joshie is firstly that he is a little boy, and it is easier to make children better, and also that he has a kind of leukaemia which the doctors DO know how to sort out. And they accept it, both of them, that is enough. No need for further explanation: Josh is lucky, he has something different, that question has been answered. I learn a lot from the way they absorb something, ponder on it for just enough time, and then let it go.

So often I find myself preparing to continue when Ollie asks something, but he has his answer, it's dealt with and now he can move on.

We also spend some time talking through how he might feel if any parents or older kids at school approach him in the playground and ask about Josh (this has never happened). He told us he liked what we had told him about the best doctors, so he committed those three phrases to memory and said he would answer like that if anyone asked. We also add in a bit about how Josh didn't catch his leukaemia, and no-one can catch it from him, in case other kids get a bit 'eurgh yuck germs' about it.

I have vivid memories of being in the primary school playground and my mum had bought me some (absolutely vile) chunky, what I can only describe as 'crumpet shoes'. They were brown, no laces or buckles, almost like a soft brown leather clog, with sort of waxy soles that were really flexible, they were kind of like the shoe-offspring of a hippy and a nerd. In fact they were almost like a more crumpety version of the slip-on Doc Martens, but DMs were cool in the next decade, and besides I was in primary school. No doubt they were spectacularly good for my feet. At my primary school in the mid-80s girls wore glittery or patent, pink, sparkly t-bar shoes with white ankle socks, or pixie boots if it was raining. And for a whole week, two girls marched with linked arms in their beautiful, glittery shoes around the perimeter of the playground, perfectly in time with each other, and each time they passed me they both pointed at my shoes and shouted, "EEURGH!" and laughed. Round and round they went, "Eurgh!" "Eurgh!" I have no idea what I was doing, I make it sound like I was just standing still, a big brown-clothed lump with turd shoes waiting to be sneered at, but I don't think I was particularly miserable; this was the same school where we played kiss chase, and I even got married to Oliver, and Tanya brought in a veil for me to wear on the big day. He gave me a ring. We were seven. We had 'dates' after school where we made tunnels for our pet hamsters out of ladybird books. Awesome. Clearly the "Eurgh!" girls didn't irreparably damage my street cred. But I remember it, and I want to protect my seven year old son from anything like it.

This was by no means the sum total of the school bullying I endured; some pretty hefty teenage-girl stuff (I could write an entire book on that) changed me fundamentally and left me with an admittedly skewed sense of how terrifically important it is to fit in, and now it strikes me that having no hair and being known as the 'sick boy' (or the sick boy's brother for that matter) is a major red flag. I calm myself by thinking how lucky it is that Josh is only five; at this age they are barely out of preschool and incredibly accepting. But also the school themselves are all over it; right from the day he was diagnosed they offered unswerving support, going a long way out of their way to make sure we as a family, not just Josh, were as comfortable as we could be at school, were protected from unnecessary stress and worry, and had all the support we needed. Over time, teachers who I have never met and aren't involved with either of our schoolboys approach me and introduce themselves, say how much they think of us and offer unswerving support. We are unbelievably lucky – the hospital team also tell us this is not the case for every child, we clearly have an excellent school. My heart swells and beats that little bit more strongly on days like these. These people have got our backs, even the ones we don't know about.

It is genius how the school fosters this environment of kindness and concern; I don't know the magic formula but I'd guess that it filters down from the principal and the teachers, and the perfect example of this is The Robot. Josh starts Big School during Protocol M, which is spectacularly fortunate timing: although he has no hair, he's lost all his steroid weight from the first protocol, he is in a good mood (again unaffected by steroids), and is only allowed to be discharged from hospital once he is essentially feeling ok, so if we are home, it means he is in good shape for someone in the midst of intensive chemo. He gets a couple of months at school before vanishing for a while for the next protocol, a nasty one. But at the start of the school year his amazing teacher discovers a wonderful foundation who provide 'telepresence robots' for children who have to miss a lot of schooldays due to serious or life-threatening illness. It is incredible; Josh can sit on his hospital bed, or at home if he is well but his blood counts are too low for him to be among other kids, and connect to the class so that his little head is on the screen of the robot's head, and he can see and hear them all through the camera, but best of all he can drive it! So when Mrs M says, "Story time! Everyone on the mat!" he can drive it along with Annabel and Clementine and Liam and Digby and Fraser all giggling and jostling, to the mat, turn it to face Mrs M and listen to the story!! And then he can drive it back to his desk, see the whiteboard, follow the lesson plan…

The school is massively excited about this, and at the next whole school assembly Mrs M takes the robot up onto the stage and shows it to the whole school. I wasn't there so I have no idea what she said (and both boys did their standard, "Umm, she said this is the robot…" when I try to prise detail out of them), but several friends text later that night to say their kids came home from school bubbling with excitement about the cool robot. Josh has done four days at school and already his leukaemia is creating positivity and a cool, upbeat vibe through the school. Now that is how you foster an environment of positivity and kindness! I go from niggling worries about 'sick boy' to a strange pride for my 'robot boy'. Again, awesome.

So we get underway with Protocol M – four admissions of high doses of methotrexate. Each of these is an estimated four to five day hospital stay. We arrive in the evening, Josh is hooked up through his central line to 'double maintenance' through the night (this is basically just a huge amount of fluids to start his kidneys flushing effectively, as far as I can tell), and once they are happy that he is alkaline enough (wee bottles abound, five or six at a time under his bed, changed constantly and arriving fresh and steaming from the industrial sterilizer) they begin a twenty-four hour methotrexate drip. Once the twenty-four hours is up, he is given precisely timed doses of rescue drugs to help his little body recover and prevent any lasting damage. I am sure there is way more to it than that, but this is the basic outline. His levels are measured through blood tests from his line every few hours, and when the methotrexate level is below an agreed number (in our case 150) he can go home. This last bit is called 'clearing the methotrexate'. Lots of the children on the oncology ward are having this treatment at any one time; it isn't only used for leukaemia patients, and everyone has different doses and different clearing levels to aim for.

So the pressure's on: the longer he takes to clear, the longer we stay in hospital. I decide that my five year old's competitive streak needs to be nurtured and developed rather aggressively at this point. A fellow mum gives me a tip that the more food and drink you can cram into them in the first twenty-four hours, the more their body gets to work weeing and pooing it out, and therefore also flushing out the methotrexate. And this is a hefty chemo – after those first twenty-four hours he is unlikely to have much appetite. In addition, the anti-emetics are pumped right up and additional ones appear on his medication chart to stop him feeling appallingly nauseous. And happy ninja dance, for us, they work! He vomits briefly in the third and fourth admissions once in the morning as the twenty-four hours come to a close: pitiful, horrible, miserable. And yet it strikes me at this point that this is the first time he has actually vomited purely from chemo nausea (as opposed to anxiety or stress); the magic anti-emetic wafers really do the trick with all the other chemo he has had.

We are now around four months in, and my brain is beginning to function on two paths: one relatively sane, the other always teetering on the brink of hidden hysteria. At one of these admissions Scott drops us off at sunset as usual in the 'drop zone', we check in with Josh's little ride-on wheelie rattling deafeningly along the corridors, trailing a giant blue dinosaur pillow, me weighed down by our Redkite bag crammed with essentials for the next four days (four if we are lucky and he clears fast). We enter through the swing doors of the ward, sterilizing our hands ineptly (this is all pre-Covid) with the squirty pink stuff, ready for bed already. Here we are again, cocooned in the safe zone, fresh-faced nurses with their ready smiles and trolleys of really quite nice food dotted around, fellow parents softly flip-flopping in their slippers up and down the corridor to and from the parents' room... Regular, muffled beeps come from some of the rooms, the lights are low, bedtime on the ward. Who will be our roommates tonight we wonder?

Josh marches up to the nursing station and eyeballs the nurse in charge tonight. We know her, like all of them she is awesome.

"Hello!" she says.

"Hello," he answers seriously, "I'm Josh. I'm here for my methotrexate."

At least he didn't shorten it to meth. I don't know whether to laugh or cry.

She bursts into peals of laughter, he does his cheekiest smile and happily trots off behind her, dinosaur and wheelie in tow, as she leads us to our room. My brain shifts into hysterical mode: Josh is a tiny, well-spoken addict demanding his weekly order of highly illegal substances from his dealer. His voice echoes in my head and morphs into Grant Mitchell's voice - gravelly and growly, "And giss a side o' that falinic acid as well will ya...I'm good for it, and some leucovorin as well. Good shit that, protects uh liv-ah dunnit." The opening bars of the Eastenders theme tune thump into my head as I plod down the corridor. I am going completely mad.

Despite the occasional vomit, these admissions are not the nightmare I had envisaged. By now Josh and I are bonded, we are in our zone, we know enough of our one hundred and fifty new friends to feel comfortable on the ward, and I am wearing my gratitude cloak day and night and marvelling at the system at work. I think there is also a strange sort of energy in the resignation and acceptance that this must be done. Like a thread of galvanized steel running through me and Josh; we have to do this, we don't have any option not to, so get on with it. I make the conscious decision not to dwell on the unpleasantness of the many, many possible side effects of this drug – the staff know how to handle it, they are making him better, both on the huge scale, the wider arc of his two year journey, but also at each of these single admissions with the rescue meds and the monitoring of toxin levels.

So I actively decide not to dread the hospital stays; they are tough, unknown in some respects, daunting yes, very. But that thread of steel is there. And we get really stuck into the 'how fast can you clear it' game. We race to the bottom of our water bottles (I think this may have been the most hydrated phase of my life thus far), we take turns to eat mouthfuls of spinach pie dunked in ketchup, or hot chips – all painstakingly separated on the plates as Josh himself is severely cytotoxic right now and I mustn't get so much as a dot of his saliva on my fork. Very weird. They also give him doses of a drug which makes him wee loads, and I mean loads, to help flush it out too, and I am up and down like a jack in the box holding his wee bottle for him while he jiggles around standing on his bed, lines wiggling, neon yellow wee slowly fading to clear as the day wears on… And the rest of the world chugs on outside. We are suspended in our bubble, our neon yellow bubble.

We bond with our roommates, they join in with our elation when he clears his MTX in a record twenty-four hours at one admission. Josh gets horrible stomach pain for a couple of hours, but it fades and is manageable with the help of Lego. During one of the stays a drum kit appears in the playroom, the electronic sort with headphones. Barefoot, with stick legs poking out from his baggy shorts, Josh shuffles across the corridor with his various lines trailing and tangling around his pole, and settles himself on the stool. Headphones on, drumsticks in hand, he goes for it. Nutter. This boy has a real nutter streak in him. I thought he'd be lying in major discomfort for these four days, not whacking a drum kit with all his might. I absolutely love the idea that some of the teenage patients could really let rip on this, let out some frustration and fury. It must be so heart-breakingly awful for teenagers. I don't see any teenagers drumming while we are there, I hope they did at some point.

CHAPTER 17

Day 155

The weeks tick by and we are back into outpatient phase. I develop an addiction to plain black overalls / jumpsuits / dungarees. Not the 1970s denim sort, but wide-legged kind of Japanese utility style, with a Breton stripe t shirt or a sleeveless grey tank top underneath. I wear them with energetic bright white plimsolls and bounce around smiling, or, if I'm feeling confident, with ankle boots and a big bright scarf - they make me feel spectacularly and irritatingly capable, sort of functional and not like I have made an effort (they have to be the most comfortable item of clothing I have ever worn), but still like I haven't quite lost the will to get dressed. It's pathetic, but looking ok, managing to find the minutes to do my hair and put on mascara matters more than it ever did previously; when I can no longer find the energy to do this then I have succumbed to this cancer hell. That is not going to happen. It crosses my mind how horribly materialistic or vain this must make me, but I am past caring now; I am still figuring out each day how I can cope, and anything that makes me look in the mirror and think 'you don't look like a mad person' is a good thing. So. Mascara and hair straighteners travel with me (although no straighteners at the hospital stays, that would be frankly ridiculous, I am not that insane). Sometimes I get Josh or Ollie to pick my outfit for the day. They always go for the bright stuff – a 1950s style dress with pineapples all over it becomes a favourite – and I figure this is absolutely worthwhile. Ollie chooses my earrings every time we stay away from him; the chemo nurses get used to seeing me with silver rabbits dangling from my ears. We love rabbits in this family.

Five months in... New chemos, new protocols, new side effects, new logistics to work out. I continue to take Josh to his appointments, Scott works, brings home the bacon. This was our arrangement; how could it possibly not be? Albie gets teeth, Scott gets tired, Ollie gets a cough, family life continues like a galaxy swirling steadily around the epicentre of leukaemia and its associated fears and its total incompatibility with normal routine.

At a certain point the vibe in the clinic seems to change; by 9am it is packed when before we would often be the first or second people there. Our team tells us there has been a flood of new diagnoses. Children with still-glossy hair, wide-eyed mums staring straight ahead trying not to scream, haggard dads with no idea what to say to their wives, straggling siblings mercifully glued to ipads... New Caledonians fill the waiting room some days, cheery, robust French chat bounces to and fro, chemo nurses lapse gamely into jolly, Aussie-accented French. I could join in but find myself smiling from the sidelines, it's not my moment.

One day I find myself talking to a mum with lilac hair whose son was diagnosed with leukaemia a couple of months after Josh. Again I hear myself with astonishment;

I sound like someone who Knows What She Is Doing. I am reassuring her, laughing about funny things nurses have said, sharing our general horror, and whenever there is a pause in the conversation filling it with a flat-yet-companionable, "Yeah it is just so shit." Around the same time the staff all start talking to us slightly differently; taking less time to check I am coping ok. No-one calls Josh 'buddy' or 'little man' any more; he is Josh, and he is greeted by many of them with a massive hug and a joke. Anaesthetists can somehow tell it's ok for them be loud and jokey, he isn't about to burst into tears. Chemo nurses hook him up merrily and talk about which of the animals from Sing they want to marry. "The gorilla! I mean I know he's a bit hairy but just you WAIT until you hear him SING!" Most excitingly, our team start mentioning 'the end of the intensive bit'. This is phenomenal; one minute we were crashing through shell-shocked hell and now suddenly we seem to be more than halfway through the intensive phase, and talking about his central line coming out in a few more months. Things are planned way, way ahead, but still, they are planning it! My eyes begin to gleam with newfound motivation. I describe it to friends as feeling maybe like Everest Camp 4: you have climbed so damn far, and now you are about to start the summit assault. There are horrible obstacles to overcome before you get there like the Hillary Step, but the summit is in sight.

The obstacles in our case are that this third chunk of the intensive seven months is the roughest; as far as I can see from the 'menu' it is a cocktail of everything he has had so far all mashed up with a few extra ones thrown in for good measure. This combination, on top of the cumulative effect of months of massive chemo doses, mean the likelihood of unexpected admissions and infections gets higher and higher. We have had a really smooth run, I now know, and they warn us that if the wheels are going to fall off, this is the protocol where they will, possibly "spectacularly". This from the oncology god who upgraded us from 'unremarkable' to 'boring'. So that now-familiar sense of doom and dread sets in.

And yet the end of the intensive bit is in sight! Elation and motivation to get us through the nasty protocol. And Joshie is strong, in good shape, just how they want him to be. However there is a weird dichotomy going on here. We are utterly immersed now, Josh and I, in this world, in this fear, we are confronted with paediatric oncology constantly. We sit every few days in the clinic or on the ward surrounded by children who are at various stages of various cancers. Some are newly diagnosed and still look well. But some are absolutely pitiful to see. 'Confronting' really is the only word for it. Rake-thin, unable to walk, discoloured skin, naso-gastric tubes, central lines placed I assume strategically to target brain tumours, scars, vision problems, slumped... Many are in wheelchairs. Parents look harrowed, far more harrowed than me. Josh and I must look almost guiltily robust.

And the dichotomy is that Scott, the other half of the parent duo, isn't being confronted by this. Cracks start to open up in our relationship. They warned us this would happen at the start, they gave us handbooks and literature all about the toll it takes on a marriage, counseling helplines, they were blunt. They also told me emphatically that I absolutely must not take Josh to every appointment, and that it was essential that Scott brought him to some. I nodded politely, inwardly thinking, 'Ha! Like he is patient enough to sit through these days... He's better off pitching to clients and feeling good about himself. And besides when we stay in hospital his back won't handle a pull-out armchair. It has to be me.' We didn't exactly bat the advice away, but we thanked them and then we sat down and figured out how we would make everything work. Actually scrap that, we figured out how we would survive, we were firefighters in the flames. But it turns out they know best. Of course.

I speak to a fellow mum on the phone whose son has recently come out the other side of his leukaemia. She has separated from her husband and moved out of their sprawling family mansion with her two sons; her husband didn't get involved after the initial diagnosis, he immersed himself in his professional life in order to cope, he had to in order to support the family financially. She was full of resentment at his lack of engagement and they couldn't fix it.

This stops me in my tracks. Holy moley we are sailing dangerously close to the wind; are Scott and I hurtling towards that? Small things make me flash with intense anger towards Scott when he is home at the weekends; he doesn't think, he stacks big plates on top of little plates in the drawers, what is WRONG with him?! Why do I have to ASK him to do really basic stuff, why do I go out and come home at 3pm to find none of the boys has been given lunch? He lies in the hammock on a Saturday afternoon playing with Albie while I am putting on laundry, going to buy groceries, making food, hanging out laundry, mixing someone a chocolate milk, picking up stuff from all over the floor... and I was the one who was up four times last night with Albie. He says, "But darling I mowed and strimmed all the lawns this weekend, I did all that for you!" WTF, what planet is he on? I do not give a flying monkey's bum about the lawns. I care about making sure Joshie doesn't die, and making sure all our kids eat, and that Scott and I stay mentally sane. When I try this response it doesn't work. He thinks I am venting, over-dramatizing. Men are from Mars, women are from Venus. This is really, really hard.

Suddenly our practical decision looks ridiculously naïve and simplistic. Instead of this:

'Scott works hard to keep his business flourishing and bring in an income to pay our mortgage so I can devote myself to supporting Josh in his battle.'

It now feels like this:

'Scott gets to go to work and hang out with adults as though everything is normal, god he even stays away from us for most of the week, he isn't seeing what I see day in, day out, we live in different worlds and he doesn't understand the first thing about what is involved in keeping the family going…'

We are SO on the same track as that fellow mum, it hits me really, really hard when I see it. This is frightening stuff, big stuff. Scott is my second husband and I don't want to get divorced twice. I like the Finnish wedding vows where you apparently promise to try to respect, to try to love, to try to honour each other for ever and ever until death us do part etc. They warned us, they told us this could happen. I am embarrassed at how bloody textbook we must be. Embarrassed but also oddly reassured. If we are textbook then that means there must be a textbook fix, a known strategy to sort it out. I cross my fingers and start seeing a psychotherapist. So does he. We have joint sessions.

In the middle of the fifth month one of our chief nurses, a fabulous, crazy-in-the-best-way Glaswegian asks me outright how our marriage is faring. I drop the perma-cheer and tell her straight it is hard. She takes over and basically says almost word-for-word what I was about to say. She even moves her hands and arms in the same motion I had done the day before when trying to explain how I felt to Scott – she puts her hands flat in front of her, together, and then moves them out and apart as though she is starting to do breaststroke, so they get further and further apart. Yes, that is our daily life right now. This must be old hat for her, she has seen this and knows exactly what needs to happen now. She gives me a very blunt, non-negotiable instruction:

Scott has to bring Joshie for his next couple of appointments: he has to take the full day off work to do this, to get him there at the right time, sign him in, wait, do bloods, wait, get Joshie his snacks, chat, not chat, nod at other parents, see the doctor, write down the blood counts for that day, listen to the doctor's instructions for the next week, give Donna on the front desk the booking form for the next appointment, wait, go through to the chemo room, sit with Josh while he is connected, hear Joshie's rapport with his nurses, acknowledge the other parents, see the other kids, dammit be CONFRONTED by the other kids, share in the camaraderie, share in the horror, watch them wheeling child after child out of the general anaesthetic room, see how busy and friendly and gorgeous the staff are, watch the minutes tick down on the chemo pole, get him more snacks, connect to the hospital wifi, fend off Josh's constant requests for new Lego kits, make himself a cup of tea from the nurses' boiling water tap, find the milk in the fridge in the other room, take Joshie for a wee in the loo down the corridor while he is connected to his lines without running over the tubes with the wheels of the pole, flush the loo twice with the lid shut because he is mid-chemo, wash his hands and Joshie's hands with antibacterial disinfectant, walk him back with his beeping pole to his armchair, pick up some extra central line dressings when the drip is finished, gather up all their things, wait while Joshie hugs his favourite nurses, wave to Donna on the front desk, get the car parking ticket validated, take Josh for a final cytotoxic wee in the bathrooms near the main hospital exit, walk back to the car park (Josh always remembers what level and where we parked so Scott doesn't have to do that), and get him home before he needs another (still toxic) wee.

Yes, Scott needs to do that, she says. I stutter out something about how he sometimes has to go to Melbourne for meetings... No, she says, this is the moment to do it as the more time goes by the more likely Josh will be admitted with a fever as the effects of the chemo are cumulative by this point, and then Scott won't be able to stay overnight because of his back, and he needs to take action now. I also suggest Scott comes with me. Now she is really firm, like, scary Glaswegian firm: no. She says it quite directly in broad Glaswegian with a strict shake of her head: naw, naw. If he comes with me he will be a bystander while I do everything and think of everything. The whole point is that he has to think of it all himself and be responsible for all of it himself. This is my first introduction to the phrase: the Mental Load. I am not allowed to show him how things work.

I am nervous about broaching this with Scott; will he bridle against being told what to do? He hates being told what to do. He is one of those men where you have to make subtle suggestions and hints and look away and bite your tongue with impatience while he arrives at the answer himself, and then, with great glee and mirth, exclaim oh well done you!! What a great idea, how clever to think of that!? However I have to be brave about it, if I am feeling so dreadful then the chances are he is too, whether or not he has been open with himself and his psychotherapist about it. He isn't at home (of course) but this can't wait until we sit down together at the weekend so it has to be a phone conversation, and in fact it doesn't take much to get him to understand. I explain the conversation with our favourite Glaswegian and frame it as a direct instruction from her, not from me, and when he hears how predictable this is he clicks into action. I give him a list of days he needs to be out of the office, he gets on with it. Not a whiff of his usual melodramatic 'we will go out of business if I am not physically there every single day'. I heave a silent sigh of relief. We have a chance at this, we have a chance. We are approaching the cliff edge but we haven't yet launched ourselves blindly off it like lemmings.

CHAPTER 18

During our first week in hospital when Joshie was diagnosed, Albie, then eleven months old, threw up spectacularly on me while I was talking to a nurse. Both grannies were there, and they helped me get to the shower room where we hosed off Albie and I rinsed the vomit out of my cleavage (I still had one then as I was breastfeeding, now it has just gone away 'without even saying goodbye' to quote Leslie Mann in This Is 40). A fellow ward mum knocked on the bathroom door and stuck her head in to offer me whatever I needed, baby clothes, fresh clothes for myself, towel, whatever... She looked about half my age and had her baby on her hip, a beautiful round-faced little girl only a couple of months older than Albie, and was trailing chemo lines from her daughter's cute, podgy tummy and manoeuvring the iv pole expertly. She was so kind. We were so obviously cut from different cloth and yet I never felt like she saw me as anything other than a fellow mum, she didn't judge me, she was my first experience of the straight-down-the-line nature of the cancer mum bond. I don't know if it exists for the men; I haven't sat and cried or shared the fear and horror with any oncology dads at this point, although one dad who shared our room did cry a bit when I told him how Joshie was diagnosed which was beautiful, really, this big football-shirt-wearing hulk of a man just being open and honest with his emotions. So this young mum, the vomit-support-mum, and I are bonded. She gave me tips on how to get to sleep in hospital, told me about the naughty snack menu which is on a separate piece of paper to the standard hospital catering sheet, told me which food restaurants would deliver when you got so sick of hospital food you needed a Nando's... She knew her stuff. And her baby girl had a tumour in her stomach, a big one.

Fast forward a few months and I receive a text from her that starts, 'Hi everyone...' and my stomach clenches. They tried everything; there is nothing else they can do, her tumour has grown back aggressively and they have found many more. She has been moved into palliative care where they are making her comfortable. We still hope for a miracle.

A couple of weeks later she texts again to say her baby daughter is now in a better place, free from pain and suffering. I am standing in the kitchen stirring something and I drop the wooden spoon, the grief is a physical punch. I fizz with rage and emotion. My Joshie is strong, he is a lion cub. This little girl was a BABY. This is too cruel. It is too much. She had the bluest eyes, she was the cover girl on the end of year edition of the oncology newsletter we all get. And for her picture they didn't choose a posed, magazine-ad style photo of her, they used the most gorgeous character shot of her where her entire face is creased up, wrinkled nose, in a properly cheeky grin, leaning into the camera and probably squealing, she looks delicious. She would march into the clinic and stick her squidgy arm out to the gorgeous ladies on the front desk demanding a lolly, she knew how the system worked. Her little body. It is over, she is over. I think there can be few things more genuinely, truly tragic than a little coffin. That, and the agonizing music of Ravel's Pavane Pour Une Enfante Défunte. It is just heart-collapsingly painful.

Out of nowhere, not having heard it for at least ten years, Dido's 'See The Sun' starts up one day a few weeks later on my playlist, and my eyes burn with tears and I double up, heaving and gasping for breath – the lyrics, probably about a break up, fit the unbearable agony of losing a baby girl so perfectly it takes my breath away. It is incredible how songs from decades ago when life was so easy, so 'lite', take on such a new meaning, new weight. I imagine many people might feel the same, the more of life we accumulate under our belts, the more we gain perspective and the knocks and scrapes of living a full, human life. Do the songwriters and the musicians know this, though they are often so young? They write songs with broad appeal in order to sell records, but wow when you find the song that fits your pain, or your friend's pain… what power. I had a friend at university whose phd was all about why it is that music, which is sound, not a solid thing you can touch, can make us feel a physical sensation. How do our nerves do that, how does it convert auditory stimuli into neurological activity and thus bodily experience? I didn't read his phd. I should have, he was an eccentric genius with a crazy, shockingly loud laugh.

Another beautiful little girl loses her battle during this same week. She was seven, she had a very rare brain tumour, her mother is a friend of a friend. This world we are walking in now, the stakes are high and brutal. I marvel at the horror, the sheer pain of life and death, again at the feeling that this is all happening while the rest of the normal world continues on around us. Another song looms, Dixie Chicks' Streets of Heaven, they sing about how it must be crowded on the streets of heaven, why do they have to take her now, and in the song she is a seven year old girl... This one I can't even sadly hum along to in the car, tears pour down my face at the lyrics and the perfect, gutsy, almost-breaking voice, it is too much. It is just too much. I feel like little tiny shards of my heart break off for these too-soon deaths. We carry these small people in our hearts. Little notches. I wonder how the parents heal, and remember a chance conversation early one morning in the local wholefood store where I blurted out to the shop assistant that I had a son with leukaemia, and she replied with a sad smile that she had lost her young daughter a few years ago. We hugged, wiped tears, laughed self-consciously at the weirdness of crying with a stranger at 9.30am in the morning after school drop off. And I will never forget how she said with a peaceful smile that they were so lucky to have had her. Humans are incredible. I have heard that you never get over it, but you get used to it.

CHAPTER 19

Day 162

The marathon, this onslaught of toxicity for which we are beyond grateful, continues into the next protocol and we find ourselves back again in the thick of the steroid fog. He is unrecognizable, I have lost my boy to dexamethasone this time. In the first protocol at the start it was prednisone, this time round the effects are very similar but feel condensed, plus as well as bouts of road rage they warn us, correctly, that he will be more teary and generally just sad. It must feel so appalling for him – once the steroids have taken hold I pause and contemplate him, he is enormous, properly huge. Matchstick arms and legs stick out from an absolute barrel, the five year old scale equivalent of being overdue with a third pregnancy. His enormous, taut, hard tummy is divided up by blue and pink veins under the skin, frantically, desperately pumping his strange, toxic blood around his little body. Bizarrely I think of Ordnance Survey maps from my childhood: B-roads criss-crossing the English countryside, blue rivers winding across counties, contour lines marking tors and fells and escarpments. His neck has thick, soft rolls of fat and fluid bloat, his chin has completely vanished, his mouth is a tiny downturned rosebud, his eyes and nose are squished in the middle of a great, round, soft, moon-head. He still has his hair but it will fall out soon. His face reminds me of a cartoon starfish, or the underside of a stingray, piggy little features all bunched together. His eyes have lost their characteristic sparkle, they are dull, and his face, his whole demeanour, oozes effort. His cheeks must weigh a ton; smiling is rare and hard work. The bottom of his face is markedly wider than the top of his head.

He tries to haul himself up stairs, but one of the chemos he is having alongside the steroids, our old friend Vinc, causes nerve pain in his legs so I have to carry him. Despite being untoned and more like a gym slug than a gym bunny, I am usually pretty strong and can sweep him up in my arms, legs dangling, without much effort. But now I have to brace myself, legs apart, lift with my thighs, take it one step at a time…this is a whole different ballgame. When I lie next to him in bed I study his face and see that even his temples are fat – the patch between the outer corner of his eye and his hairline is puffed up; I can poke it gently and it podges in and out. This is some drug.

It's meant to do this, the oncology god describes him as a 'fine specimen' of a little boy on dex, which is reassuring. And yet, looking at my son, my baby, and not seeing the person you know, is once again incredibly bizarre. His temperament is off the wall; he has become utterly obsessed by Lego, possessed by it even. It consumes his attention completely, he manages to immerse himself in it to the exclusion of everything else. My mum wants to write to Lego and tell them how vital it is to his tolerance of this hell, but I think they probably know this. Children's wards all over the world are peppered with creations and displays and I would bet a lot of money that most hospital janitor's vacuum cleaners have at least ten pieces of Lego in every single bag of dust they suck up. He wants more and more, new sets, new kits, he consumes the stuff, bloody Lego keep bringing out new ones, if he takes a break from Lego building he spends it watching youtube videos of other people building Lego. He doesn't make big demands or shout or become angry, he is just quietly heartbroken when we say he can't have another new one. It is awful; they told us this would happen, that small things would render him incapable of normal behavior and trigger intense sadness. I stare at the big, fat tears rolling silently down his big, fat cheeks. This is not Josh, this is dex, this is an unnatural, chemical suffering.

Scott is quick and decisive about what we have to do: if ever there was a time to indulge him, this is it. It goes against our usual parenting habits to spoil our boys, but we have a credit card, and this is what it is for. This is arguably survival, life is not normal, nothing is normal any more. I take Ollie out for one of our therapy milkshakes and explain carefully that Joshie's behavior is not how he will be forever, it is the medicine that he's taking which is making him behave strangely. He seems to get it right away, taking over from me and talking about how Josh cries at tiny incidents and shouts at dear little seventeen month old Albie, things he would never normally do. I tell him that we have decided to buy a few more Lego kits to help all the family get through the next couple of weeks while he is finishing the dex, but this is not how things are going to be forever, and Ollie does a fantastic job of looking appropriately concerned about the serious subject matter, and yet simultaneously restraining himself from falling off his chair with excitement at the prospect of New Toys. I sigh inwardly and shove away the voice in my head chastising me for giving in to materialistic demands, and financial idiocy as we are stretched thin now, no just piss off alright, this is big, this is bigger than parent guilt, bigger than idealistic ethics of instilling good values in your kids, this is leukaemia, this is cancer. Just shut up, chastising voice, and let me take the easier option with my credit card. God knows there are enough hard things to deal with right now.

So dexamethasone is renamed Legomethasone in my head, and he builds away furiously, on the floor at home, on the table during chemo iv drips, on his bed, on the sofa...frowning intently, huge cheeks pushed into a great rosy hefty pout. He swiftly becomes a pro, flying through the kits for 8 - 14 year olds and eating the Ninjago stuff for breakfast. I find tiny dragon's claws, thumbnail-size pizza slices, tyres, argh the tyres, EVERYWHERE. I give in; this is my life, this is my house. One day it will all be serene and I will light my Danish candles in dust-free, glass storm lanterns again, and the boys will keep their stuff in their stinky rooms instead of all over every room in the house.

Speaking of stinky, kind of hilariously (you have to find things to laugh about or you would go mad) the dex also seems to make him fart like a trooper. Fortunately for me I have always found farts very, very funny, though ideally the ones that make a noise. I still start to laugh faintly hysterically at the memory of an ex-boyfriend's rather formal father bending over to help me load the dishwasher in his beautiful Georgian vicarage, and accidentally letting out a short, pert fart perilously close to my face. He apologized profusely and one of his many sons let out a guffaw of incredulous hilarity; farts are brilliantly funny. I also sang in chapel choirs for several years at university and, as all choristers know, a well-timed, perfectly-pitched fart can transform even the blandest of evensongs into a half hour of snort-stifling, tear-rolling, team-bonding awesomeness.

Unfortunately for me at the moment however, Joshie is teary and vulnerable enough to need to sleep in my bed through this phase (I snort with derision at the memory of those articles you see on parenting forums where people inexplicably judge other parents for co-sleeping, oh you lucky, lucky people who can wonder about whether it is 'the right thing' to sleep next to your child) and this means I frequently climb in under the blankets next to him and almost faint at the great cloud of steroid-gas that hangs over our bed. I keep a massive box of matches in the bedroom, and scented candles become an essential household item rather than a lovely indulgence.

And there is something particularly comic about Josh farting while he is so bloated and huge – I honestly wonder if at some point he might do the mother of all farts and slowly and steadily deflate to his normal size. He expanded so fast, in the space of a few days, surely one good expulsion could sort it out? We giggle uncontrollably about this together, he likes the idea of being pricked with a pin, preferably in his tummy button, and zooming around the room as the air whizzes out, like a balloon emptying, making a wonderful whoopee cushion noise as he flies from corner to corner...

As well as being generally bloated and enormous, he is also absolutely starving all the time. One Sunday, at 'peak Dex', I spend two hours straight standing in the kitchen making food for him, non-stop, no exaggeration. He requests chicken, I chop up a rotisserie chicken. He inhales both legs and then asks for one of the breasts. Five minutes later, "Mum I'm so hungry can I have some tortilla crisps please?" Deliver a small bowl of crisps.

"Fanks." (We are apparently too fat at this point to pronounce the sound 'th'.)

"Can I now have some carrot sticks with mayonnaise

but loads of mayonnaise please?"

I chop three Aussie-scale carrots (i.e. carrots which look to this British mum as if they are on steroids themselves) and dollop mayo.

Five minutes later, "Is there any of that roast beef left?"

And again, "Can I now have a chocolate milk?"

Five minutes later, "Can you warm up some sausage rolls? Actually can you drive to Gumnut Patisserie to get me a chicken pie?"

And so it goes on. We take little bowls of pasta to bed for when he is 'starving' in the night, I buy a ready-roast chicken a day. I find myself pacing the supermarket aisles every day, sometimes twice a day, searching out his latest request. I can report that sadly nowhere in our local town sells proper German giant pretzels.

And it's the psychological idea of eating, not just the act of eating any old thing. One particular day he checks every few minutes obsessively that we are indeed definitely having fish fingers for lunch as he has requested, I reassure him time and time again, and then Albie's toddler playlist comes on and the Wiggles start singing about hot potatoes and suddenly a little voice appears at my hip, asking innocently and without a trace of embarrassment, "Mum? Do we have any potatoes? I think I really need some mashed hot potatoes. I don't mind if you have already started making the fish fingers but I do really want hot potatoes."

This is one hungry boy.

I compare notes with other mums at the clinic who describe exactly the same experiences, although one has the added complication that her son's taste buds have changed because of the chemo. We wipe tears of loving, bewildered laughter from our eyes as she describes how her son is adamant that he wants prawns, all day every day, and loads of them, but whenever he tastes them he is steroid-furious that they taste of ham. More prawns are cooked in case these ones taste right...they don't. But they HAVE to be prawns. Just not ham-tasting prawns. And so it goes on.

We are parents of mini, hopefully-temporary junkies. Bloated ones. Who do not resemble the children we know. Very, very weird.

This transformation is a true, complete one. He went from 21kg to 26kg in fourteen days, that's 5kg in two weeks! Almost a quarter of his initial body weight! For much of the time Josh's resilience, in the purest sense of the word, and his humour truly carry me along. I am like a weather-beaten old sailing yacht being blown by a wonderful steady breeze across bumpy, messy waters. There is one time when he is at his largest, top-heavy and looking like he shouldn't really be able to balance on his twiglet legs according to all the laws of physics, when he happily dashes out of our bedroom and promptly faceplants onto the carpet. For a split second he and I both freeze and then I take the lightning quick decision to see if I can make it funny. "Whoah! What happened there?!" I say with an upbeat yet hopefully sympathetic expression of surprise.

He turns round, podgy starfish-face absolutely helpless with laughter and shouts delightedly, "Aaah man!?" (not entirely sure where my boys get, 'ah man!' from), "Sometimes m'legs just do that coz they're really weak!" and he pushes himself up onto his arms and shrugs his puffy shoulders, still laughing like a happy pot-bellied half-drunk monk. I love him so much in this moment, thankfully he is facing away from me as he walks off as I can't help it, I sink down onto the bed and sit there staring in amazement at him, my jaw hanging open gormlessly. If it were me, if it were me whose legs had just given way, and I'd landed on my fat, wobbly tummy, central line lumens and clamps digging into my tired, toxic flesh, weak limbs pushing myself back up…if that were me, I am fairly sure I would crawl under my duvet and hide for the rest of the day, the week even, sobbing hot indulgent yet justified tears of self-pity and disgust at what my body had become. And yet this five year old boy just thinks it's another opportunity for a laugh.

In the most mundane moments, as the weeks grind on and on, I watch him talking, building Lego, playing with his brothers and my heart cracks over and over again at what he has become, physically. We have photos around our house of the five of us, as many families do, and when I look at the pictures of Josh he is a totally different person. He was the lucky child with the smooth, olive skin, full of sparkle and gloss, dark brown eyes crackling with character, and now those eyes are tiny slits between puffed, fluid-retaining eyelids and cheeks; when he laughs I really don't know how he can see out. It is so funny on one level, particularly as we know this second time round with the steroids that he won't be like this forever, but so painfully, exhaustingly pitiful on another. The juxtaposition of the two ways of looking at it seriously does my head in sometimes, my brain frequently short circuits and I abandon any attempt to untangle it, and just sink into 'keep going' mode. Winston Churchill's 'keep buggering on' comes to mind so very, very often.

CHAPTER 20

6 Months in

Scott has taken him to a couple of appointments without me. It starts to help us, our marriage, in infinitesimally small increments. A snide remark swallowed here, an eyeroll avoided there. Tiny gestures, and non-gestures, which begin a thawing and sow the seeds of a new appreciation, a tendril reaching out and trying to comprehend what I have been immersed in. I don't shout about it and neither does he; this is too big to be light or crass, I am immensely grateful that he doesn't come back from a long day at the hospital full of, "Oh my god I get it!" or indeed the opposite, "Well that wasn't so bad!?" No, I think he gets what needs to be done and said, this is about spending time, repetitive Groundhog Day kind of time, bedding down into the world of paediatric oncology, fighting this fight for Joshie.

I am under strict instruction to do something 'for myself' when Scott takes him to appointments. Instruction from the medical team, my psychotherapist, my friends, my mum... I'm not actually very good at treating myself to quality time. As an expat for five years in Abu Dhabi I went through phases of having the standard immaculate nails – shellac, gelish, 'greige', neon orange toes – we all did. But apart from that, and the odd extremely rare birthday spa voucher treat, I haven't really ever got properly into indulging myself. Zoning out, relaxing, yoga, meditation, spas, beauty treatments, they are all things I assumed I would be able to do later once the boys were older. Not things for now. I may have made a daft choice, albeit subliminally…

Plus I have three boys, males, little men (I always secretly hoped to have three boys, lanky and taller than me and all big feet and hands), and even though one of them is, at this point, really into cute rabbits and furry animals, my world is still essentially jam-packed with farts, bums, various different words for penises, floor is lava and ninja-sofa-leaping. Spare piece of paper lying around? We know what to draw on that! Steamed up shower screen? Let's squash this particular body part against it and see what it looks like from the other side! Parenting life for me is full of testosterone in varying concentrations, and at the risk of gender stereotyping shamefully, we don't have any unicorns in the house, not a single mermaid, there is a dearth of sequins, and I can't recall ever having to clean up glitter. And I start to realize I have let this boy-world spill over into the essentials of who I am. I have become all practical, all hands-on, strong, man-handling small, lean, wiry boys into baths. My lap has vibrated unexpectedly with many, many well-timed farts during delicious boy-cuddles. I tell myself I just don't have time to light candles and pick flowers from the garden and put them in a vase, someone will be asking me for something and besides I am Just Too Tired.

But wait, stop. This isn't right. Yes, life is full on right now, but no-one is going to die, Josh included, in the time it takes me to strike a match, light a chunky white candle in a storm lantern and stare at it while I drink a cup of hot, not tepid, earl grey tea. A quiet voice in my head reminds me that Scott regards candles as a fire risk because, well just 'because Australia'. Stuff it. I don't. I am not contemplating leaving the boys for half a day with no-one to look after them surrounded by naked flames, I am proposing to sit at the kitchen table. For five minutes.

I have completely forgotten how to care for myself. Not in a big, momentous way, but those rituals of soulful enjoyment have utterly fallen by the wayside as I blast down this highway of family life with cancer. Hell they had even gone before all this, by the time the third boy baby arrived, everything was pale blue and dinosaurs and Lego. Before I met Scott, as a single twenty-something in London, my dreamy flatmate and I christened my flat 'The Hygge'. The flat was nothing special at all: a second floor two bedroom flat on the corner of a typical Victorian London street in Stoke Newington. Heavy, slightly-damp sash windows overlooked a small park, and drunk people had noisy fights in a phone box on the street below on Saturday nights. Sirens wailed. (I am told now it has been transformed into a phenomenally chic and expensive enclave, and the little park hosts artisan markets on the weekend.)

The dreamy flatmate and I merrily channelled the Danish concept of 'hygge' positively lightyears before the media discovered it and made it mainstream - we would insist on this fact adamantly over glasses of wine in the following years. Hygge is a word that doesn't easily translate into English: it sums up a feeling or quality of contentment, snug, secure, convivial happiness, maybe with a social or aesthetic element to it, but mostly just a nourishment and kindness towards one's own soul. I hope the Danes would be ok with that explanation – it's a really hard one to define. Feeling hyggelig involves pausing to take pleasure and appreciation from the smaller things in life.

We flatmates had been to Copenhagen and decided it was basically heaven, and wanted to bring a piece of that back to our grey, rainy patch of London. My then-boyfriend told me I sounded like "a bit of a twat" when I insisted on referring to my very normal home as 'the hygge' and thought we were being completely pretentious, it really irritated him, but we didn't care, we were happy and hyggelig. We lit Diptyque candles when we came in from work, we wore snuggly cashmere jumpers in jewel-box colours, we bought armfuls of flowers from Columbia Road flower market and poured delicious glasses of wine which glinted in the snug-yet-chic candlelight while the rain slashed our urban windows. We couldn't have a roaring log fire, but it was there in essence. We made my teeny-tiny flat nice, really nice, and our souls were nourished. We loved living together.

And I am now on a planet so far away from hygge. I need to rediscover how to nurture my soul. Ever since Josh's diagnosis, friends have told me I must take time for myself, carve out micromoments, look after my own wellbeing, and I thought I was doing that, but there is a big difference between liking a 'Be Kind To Yourself' meme on Facebook and actually doing something to be kind to yourself. It's time for me to practise what I preach. I light a candle as soon as we wake up the next morning at breakfast and make the boys hot chocolate before they have their Weetbix (Ollie), nothing (Albie) and eight-slices-of-toast-with-peanut-butter-and-a   giant-bowl-of-cereal-and-an-ice-cream-smoothie-with-sneaky-chia-seeds (steroid-Josh). I instantly feel like life is a tiny weeny bit nicer. Baby steps. But I re-read that and think technically that was still mostly for them, not me. Self-care with L plates.

I dip my toes a little further into the water. A massage, a manicure, and then, courtesy of my fabulously understanding sister-in-law: a facial. And this is the game changer. I had no idea, I thought facials were just for famous people or women with lots of time and even more money! It is such a relaxing experience; I don't have to speak, the lights are dimmed, and the therapist is basically doing what I never bother to do for myself. It lasts a full hour and I get to lie flat and no-one asks me to bring them any chicken nuggets. The bed is even heated! I had no idea this existed.

I come out feeling frankly pitifully renewed; my sister-in-law had told the people at the salon about Josh and they were all just so kind and human and supportive. I feel humble and happy. And I am fabulously inspired to care for myself with better eye cream, hydrating serum, daily sunscreen...hooray for me! Something in me clicks and I begin to internalize something my psychotherapist said: the selfish choice is NOT to look after yourself. To neglect your own wellbeing means you can't care for those you love as well as you want to be able to, because you are not your best self. I know this, damn you can't get to be a 40 year old female who can read and has ears and not know this, it is emphatically not rocket science. Your own oxygen mask first blah blah... So why on earth haven't I actually done anything about it?! I am horribly guilty of saying the right thing and then just continuing scrolling on... Metaphorically. I mean I have even given friends this actual advice before. I really am utterly ridiculous. Part of me wants to berate myself furiously for being so bloody dopey, but I am not so psychologically tangled that I can't see that slamming guilt and negativity at myself at this point would be majorly counterproductive. We are aiming more for 'feelgood' than 'feelshit'. So luckily the kinder part of me wins, and I willingly give in to feeling quietly warm and reassured that I am going to be able to get Josh through this. Not just thanks to a facial, but triggered by said facial.

So bring on the hygge phase. I determine that when the time is right I will introduce our boys to hygge. I daydream about the moment. Joshie will be in the maintenance phase, so it will be winter, we'll light the firepit and toast marshmallows, I'll try to explain the idea of hygge to them, and then Scott can maybe get the telescope out and we'll all look at the moon and the Southern Cross and feel tiny but snug and content in the now. Yes! Bring it ON!!

CHAPTER 21

Day 176 – Easter Day

As time passes I lose count of the number of trips we make up and down to Sydney for his chemo. Other parents cross them off on charts, one mum of a teenage boy tells me in the waiting room that to date her son has had something phenomenal like one hundred and eighty five chemo treatments, this number of radiotherapy sessions, that number of lumbar punctures… it is staggering. One time we share a room with a lovely family whose son is having his last chemo; they have made banners and brought balloons and cupcakes, there is a real feeling of finality and celebration. I observe this with a strange mix of detached admiration and excitement, and can't help but think how tentative, how 'jinxy' I am in comparison. Even if I knew it was his final scheduled chemo I think I would still be screaming in my heart the words: if all goes well. Because what if it doesn't? And you thought that was it, but it wasn't? I'm not sure how I would stomach the rollercoaster ride of elation and heart-pounding joy, followed by absolute paralyzing horror that there is more to come. But perhaps that is exactly the point, this is about living and seizing the moment, the now, stopping to smell the victory when it is offered. Me always having in the back of my mind a little voice saying 'if, if, if…' so you don't jinx it, is that my way of holding back and not committing to the moment?

Each time we drive up and down we pass a skydiving airfield and see if we can spot any little parachutes wheeling down out of the blue. I have skydived, I know what it looks like and sounds like from up there; once you pull your chute it is truly quiet. When you jump out of the aeroplane it is all noise and hard air, rushing and roaring against your ears and face, as you take control of your brain and carry out the drill that has been hammered into you down on the ground in the training sessions. And then you pull the chute, it unfurls and you are jerked up unceremoniously as you decelerate from terminal velocity to calm parachuting speed, and suddenly all is silent. You are air, you are sky, you exist, you just are. Your harness creaks as you adjust and turn to gaze, awestruck, at the world. The land is a picture book below you, the occasional birds are your fellow travellers in this other space, for a few minutes you are not part of everything, all that down there, you are 'other'.

And so I know that as we drive along, singing, crying at the lyrics, some of the little dots we see thousands of metres above us will be looking down at us on the highway below, the little toy vehicles, maybe wondering who is in these cars and where are they going. Well, hopefully some of them are having a whale of a time just whooping adrenalin-fuelled swearwords and not thinking anything so indulgent and kind of prosaic – they are the ones probably having the best time now I think about it, living in the moment – but how weird, this infinite loop of human wondering, who are you and what is your life? And who are you and what is your life? Are you skydiving to celebrate the end of an illness, to get over a break up, to mark a birthday, to raise money? Do you skydive every day and instruct the others? Is someone holding a beer on the landing strip and is your challenge today to grab it as you land without falling over? And you down there, are you driving on your daily commute, driving to visit someone you love, driving your wife-in-labour to the hospital? Life swirls and swims overwhelmingly around us. We are so many and we are all so damn busy. Note to self: more hygge. Light the candle.

On many of these Sydney trips we stay overnight with my inlaws, basking in the love, nourishing food, clean sheets, vacuumed floors and terrestrial tv, and they live a few minutes away from a large shopping mall which has all the global brands you could possibly want. This is consumerism on a new level, and inevitably I start to save up my shopping lists for when we are there – shoes and clothes for the boys, birthday and Christmas presents, eco and ethical brands... I know my way around; I know where to find a parking spot on a rainy Saturday afternoon, I know which café does the best hot chocolate, I am this shopping mall's ninja. So fairly often, if Josh is well enough in himself on that particular day, we will arrive at the inlaws' and then I dash out to the mall. My inlaws, bless them, never comment on this extraordinary and potentially pretty antisocial habit – surely it would cross their minds that the last thing most knackered mums would want to do after driving ninety minutes alongside giant articulated lorries going at breakneck speeds on the highway is get back in the car and go to a shopping mall? But equally my mother-in-law is practical enough to know that I need to take every opportunity to tick off my to do list, and also to steal the odd hour for myself.

But there is more to it than that. It is really obvious, but it doesn't really clarify itself in my head until one day I am marching through the mall passing yet another fairy-light-festooned giraffe made of fake pine branches, brands illuminating my face with their storefront lighting as I pass, and I realize I have finished my to do list, bought my oh I don't know moisturizer and Lego kit for the next hospital stay, but I don't want to leave yet. At first I feel a wave of guilt: have I succumbed to society's 'I must consume more, I must BUY more STUFF, the little bursts of endorphins demand it' mentality? (And I am very familiar with that feeling having lived in the UAE, where millions of dollars has been very successfully poured into working out how you get human beings to stay inside a shopping mall and part with more of their money. It helps that it's fifty degrees outside.) No this is different. There is a certain true comfort in the anonymity of being among strangers, humans, and not having to speak. No-one asks me how he is. No-one comments on how well he looks, how well he is doing. No-one says anything to boost me, to support me, tells me I am doing well. I don't have to put on a bright smile and nod and acknowledge their kind (and very welcome) concern. And it's really hard to explain as I do also need that, there are days when kind words from well-meaning friends and family are the only way I avoid slumping into a heap on my bed. But it is all about balance, and I truly savour the 'face in the crowd' experiences too.

In the shopping mall I am connected to humanity, I am encountering brands that are nothing to do with Josh having cancer, just normal global population stuff: H&M, Uniqlo, Target, cafes... I am acutely aware that there is nothing novel or local about this experience and I push aside the voice that berates me for being such a stereotypical product of the 21st century, seeking comfort from brands, but that's what it is, it is just about the combination of familiarity and anonymity. I don't actually have to buy anything anyway to feel this way, it's almost as if just by being among it all some weird kind of osmosis happens and I feel less abnormal. Marketing gurus would no doubt have some fabulous psych-tech-speak for this: when a potential consumer feels confirmed and reassured by the very existence of your product (marketing nirvana, the holy grail!), but it has a very real role to play for me in this life phase. Life is continuing around me, everything has not completely spiralled out of control: if you need a pair of $2 navy and white stripy toddler socks you can still get them. Just because the rest of your life is latex gloves and double flushing after chemo and dressing changes with iodine swabs and mixing crushed white pills with honey and taking his temperature again, and again, and again…it doesn't mean the entire world has gone mad.

And I also find it comforting that according to the laws of probability, if I am walking around looking to everyone else like just another person, then there are probably loads of other people walking around, ostensibly just 'going shopping', who also have big things happening in their lives. We are humanity, we are all being stirred round and round in the mixing bowl of life by the wooden spoon.

When I look at our household spending habits I realize I actually do a fair proportion of my shopping from small, local businesses, but when I get the chance to be just a random human in a normal shopping centre, damn I'll take it.

CHAPTER 22

The last protocol of Josh's seven ish months of intensive chemo is nerve-racking. We are repeatedly told the wheels might fall off in a big way here, meaning lots of fevers, hospital stays with iv antibiotics, and therefore delays to treatment. We tiptoe around, washing hands left right and centre, sneezing into our elbows away from Josh, snapping at him not to do anything physical like climbing or sliding or running or jumping. The tension, for me, is unsustainable, and as the days creep by my mind slips into a weird stress-induced sludge where daily life seems clouded, foggy almost. I feel I am going through the motions, and we still have 4 weeks or so to get through, all being well.

A brainwave: a creative project. Nothing taxing, nothing irritating, something that will make me feel good. A quick scour on the local second hand auction sites and I find the perfect thing: a kitchen dresser (or, if you are American or Australian, a 'buffet and hutch'. This name alone makes me laugh; in England a buffet is a massive spread of free-range lunch or dinner where you keep going back for more, and a hutch is what a rabbit lives in. I like the idea of a feast for a rabbit. I digress.). It is delivered by some terrifically kind people who just turn up with it in the back of their ute, and I set to work with the paint stripper (warning on the can: may cause cancer, a wry cackle of laughter in my head) pleasingly scraping off orange varnish and sanding it back to reveal the grain of the wood. I am not a carpenter, I am not patient, I am not a perfectionist. But this is good, doing something low-stress, occupying my mind just enough to divert it from the constant 'what is about to go wrong', using my hands to make something beautiful. As I paint thick strokes of smooth, grey paint onto my feast for a rabbit, I am absorbed, calm.

It looks awesome, Scott kindly says he loves it. Ollie and Albie ooh and aah appropriately, and Josh is wonderfully furious when he finds out that the glass-windowed upper section (err, the hutch? The buffet?) actually isn't for displaying his Lego creations. He is really angry with me and huffs and snorts as he skulks around my legs while I arrange Pretty Things in it: my favourite Scandinavian cookbook, chipped white enamel jugs, teacups with rabbits standing on the handles... I need this, it is hyggelig, it is feminine, it is not tough and survivalist, it is aesthetically delicious and calm and Me. I am clawing back myself from the little-boy-and-leukaemia quagmire I have been wading through. I am going to transform the quagmire into a fast-rushing, clear glacial river of meltwater and cartwheel alongside it on the lush fat green grass under the sun. All shall be well, says T.S. Eliot. Yes the kitchen dresser has done its job.

The day after I finish my painting project, we get a letter in the post confirming the date of his 'surgical procedure' to remove his central line; it is from the regular day surgery part of the hospital, not the oncology people who we know so well. It is thrillingly impersonal, it is written as though Josh is going in to have a birthmark removed, or his adenoids out. Our oncology team confirm everything, he really is booked in to have his central line removed in a few days. We start counting down.

The day surgery computer-generated letter says weird unfamiliar things like 'please wear pyjamas on the day for the surgery and bring a set of clothes to change into afterwards'. I tell Josh and he looks absolutely aghast.

"Py-JA-mas?! What?! I am NOT wearing pyjamas!"

"But Joshie it doesn't really matter does it, your pyjamas are all really cool and you can just wear a jumper over the top, I think they just want you to be comfy…?"

"Mum, I am NOT wearing jarmies. That is really stupid. I have breaks-in-the-day all the time and I never have to wear jarmies."

Good point. We settle on a pair of tartan soft trousers with a t shirt. Could be jarmies, could be a miniature skaterboy with a bald head and serious attitude.

We drive up the day before for a blood count and appointment with the oncology god to check he is happy for the central line to come out (if there is any chance they will want to give him more iv chemo then they will leave it in), and he gives us the thumbs up. Scott, Josh and I walk out feeling giddy, Ali G's voice bounces around my head in wonder, "For real, innit?"

For the next twenty hours or so I keep peering at Josh, his little puffy face, his soft, shiny head, the bumps in his clothes where his central line jiggles around, convincing myself he is well, willing him not to spike a fever on this exciting night. He has a bath 'so I am all clean for the anaesthetist and the doctors' (it never ceases to amaze me when I hear a five year old say the word anaesthetist, I can barely say it myself) and I wash around his central line dressing quietly, this has become part of who he is, this weird silicone thing has given him life-saving medicine, I am so grateful to this inanimate object.

Josh stays cool as a cucumber all night. As I take his temperature before I fall asleep, just like every other night since he was diagnosed, it reads his usual 36.4. I kiss his forehead, stay cool little lion cub, stay cool all night.

Day 221

The day dawns, we are off. Josh is bouncing around as high as a kite, he is fasting ready for the GA and doesn't care, doesn't even want water. I am an absolute walking ball of fizzing adrenalin. If I feel like this today I cannot even begin to imagine what it will be like in another eighteen months when he rings the bell. This milestone feels enormous. Scott is calmer but behind his eyes I can see he is also fizzing, hoping, trusting all will go well.

We are in new territory once we get to the hospital, a different entrance, different check-in procedure, different staff, everything is unfamiliar. We march in beaming, I know my face is an embarrassing shade of 'puce glow' and it is going to stay this way all day, I am so excited. I can't stop smiling as we fill in the forms. Josh fidgets happily and jumps around talking loudly. We are shown through to the waiting room where I see how we stick out like a sore thumb. This is sooo weird; normally, unless we are in the oncology clinic or ward, we are the family who people look at with an almost-audible thud of pity and fear and possibly even horror, one glance at Josh and you can almost see their eyeballs flash the word 'cancer' like dollar signs in an 80s cartoon. But today we are bouncing off the walls and every other parent in the waiting room is properly, seriously stressed. It isn't funny, but it kind of is too. There is a boy with a bruised little finger holding it on a pack of ice who is playing a video game with his other hand while his dad plays another video game next to him, they don't talk to each other. There is a younger boy, maybe three years old, playing with the waiting room toys, he has a droopy eyelid and seems otherwise in excellent health to an outside observer; his mum is nervously, almost frantically, doing a Rubik's cube. A Japanese mother and son are huddled together, he looks really miserable and she is also very sad. I want to hug them, I want some of our happy, excited fairy dust to rub off on them, I want to shout, "Don't worry! You are in THE BEST place! They are great here, they are all nice and they will look after him and he will be fine! If it was more serious you wouldn't be sitting up here in the day surgery bit!" But that would clearly be extremely inappropriate and insensitive, so we play I Spy with Josh instead.

We wait and wait, sign more forms, then the anaesthetist comes by and asks us all the usual questions: food, drink, any history of asthma, any wobbly teeth...she is lovely. As she walks away one of 'our' anaesthetists from the clinic wanders past, he is an enormously tall, calm man with a deep booming voice which, I can report, instills instant calm in mothers of children about to have general anaesthetics. He recognizes Josh and we joyfully exchange hellos and quick updates; it is fantastic to see someone we know who will understand quite how exciting this day is. Next we meet our surgeon who is wearing very cool shoes and is funny. He admires Josh's hybrid pyjama-trouser solution and approves enormously (this is the only mention of pjs during the entire day, the letter was clearly overkill). In my state of high excitement I ask him if there is any chance we are allowed to keep the central line after they've removed it, as a sort of arguably gross gratitude memento. No, this is not permitted for various reasons, he says cheerfully, possibly while making a mental note that this child's mother is borderline insane. I have another of my weird moments where I feel like I know him and am probably too friendly. He is Irish and there are probably only two or three degrees of separation - I love this feeling by now, I need to come up with a word for it. A semi-stranger. It is so comforting. Not that I need comforting today, today is a day where I need to focus all my energy on not dancing or hopping or saying something inappropriate, and remembering that this is a hospital where other people are not necessarily having the best day.

Back to the waiting room, more I Spy, and then he's up next. He almost runs to the 'holding bay' bit where they go to sleep before they are wheeled into the theatre. They can still use the central line to send him to sleep and then they can switch over to a cannula (i.e. needle) when he is already under, so he won't even have to feel the cannula going in. He practically jumps up on to the bed, the huddle of anaesthetists and nurses and people around him stand back slightly in surprise at the bubble of positive energy we bring.

"Ok I'm ready, do the toothpaste!" Josh shouts with a laugh.

They love this – this is a high five personified, kids at their finest.

"It's not working I'm still awake! I'm not dizzy yet! Ok I'm dizzz…."

It is so comic, so like a scene from a mediocre movie where you would think 'yeah like it's actually going to be like that' and roll your eyes but you keep watching because it might get better. I kiss his sweet forehead for this twelfth GA, my lucky number twelve by chance, and wave them through the doors. My legs are all funny, I feel like I am stepping on a cloud, sort of floating along at the wrong speed. I am SO DAMN EXCITED. The tiny voice that used to wind me up at the start of this hellish experience doesn't get a look in – Scott is the one who adds the standard 'assuming everything goes well' to everything we say to each other while he is under. He is right, anything could go wrong, and things sometimes do, but I choose not to worry about that unless it actually happens. Me worrying about it now isn't going to help anything or change anything, so I may as well get a chai latte in my keepcup and drink it, and then, assuming there is a queue at Starbucks which there always is, he will be in recovery.

It goes well, the Irish surgeon has a brief chat with us, it was all textbook. Clever surgeons and anaesthetists with their superpowers. This time in recovery there is no spurting blood, he sits in an armchair, grumpy as usual while it wears off, and inhales almost an entire family party size bag of salt and vinegar crisps which is kind of gross, but kind of thrilling. Scott is now glowing, we are one happy threesome.

In the oncology clinic after a GA they had got to know Josh, knew he liked to get down off the bed immediately even if his legs were wobbly, knew he recovered fast and woke up strong, knew he needed observing for a short time but then we could go. Not here. This day surgery team's protocol is to keep you for four hours after a GA. FOUR HOURS. It makes total sense, they don't know how every child will react, but I hadn't really expected it to be so independent from the clinic. I smilingly and respectfully make sure they know how he usually tolerates a GA and they dutifully note it all down. He chooses a movie and we settle in for our long, boring-but-massively-excited wait to go home.

I do realize, watching other families and children in the recovery lounge, that Josh is tough and physically resilient. We knew this already of course, but seeing a large teenage boy slumped on his GA bed for at least two hours while nurses gently encourage him to wake up, and his parents chat to him, reminds me that it is not necessarily normal to get straight down off the bed and be physically able to walk and eat and swallow crisps. Who knows – I have learnt by now that there genuinely is no such thing as normal when it comes to medicine. Every child is different; Josh is having a very, very good run, he is lucky.

Once home we celebrate with a central line cake. At the risk of seeming flippant or just frankly weird, I had decided to make him a cake with an actual central line on it made of strips of sugar bootlaces poking out of the icing through a neat hole, with jelly sweets for the red and white caps on the end. 'Goodbye Central Line!' is iced around the edge in glittery blue icing. He loves it, he and Ollie bicker about who gets the jelly sweets, Albie shovels handfuls of icing 'skin' into his little mouth. It is hilarious. I have to say that although I wish our lives had been different and that I had never had to make a central line cake, I am so glad I did. I highly recommend a vaguely grotesque cake for such times. Cake feels like a good response to quite a lot of life's problems, it is celebratory, low-key, reassuringly sugary and stodgy, and also makes small children feel full and excited; it does the job.

And so we wave a thoughtful, thankful goodbye to the central line phase, and he goes into the next phase: Maintenance.

CHAPTER 23

Day 222

Maintenance is approximately eighteen months long, taking the full treatment time for Josh's type of ALL to a little over two years. He will take oral chemotherapy meds (as tablets) the whole way through: one (6MP) which he has taken previously in one of the intensive protocols alongside the iv chemo, and more of the bright yellow methotrexate which he had as a high dose iv during Protocol M. As well as these chemo tablets, he will also take an antibiotic to prevent pneumocystis pneumonia (a form of pneumonia which can occur in immuno-suppressed people), which he has taken since he was diagnosed, and will continue to take after maintenance ends as well. It is not a scary drug (err, to us!), it is widely used in the community for people with a suppressed or compromised immune system. This means quite a lot of tablets, but by this point Josh has ditched all the syringes and syrups and swills them all back with a glug of water; I take this completely for granted by now, but when I think back to those horrific early days trying to get him to take his many, many medicines, I cannot believe how far he has come in less than a year.

Handling the tablets is a bit full on, you can't touch them with bare skin or let them come into contact with anything you might then touch. We are sent home with boxes of bright blue chemo gloves which are stashed under the kitchen sink, and I develop a weird shortcut method involving putting on the gloves, then tipping the dosage of tablets into the lid of the little bottle, tipping them straight from the lid into his mouth if possible without actually touching the lid against his mouth (mixed results, but eighteen months gives you enough time to perfect this throwing-smarties-trick-inspired method) and then replacing the cap before peeling the gloves off inside out and into the bin, and wiping down the now-secure cap and bottle with an antibacterial wipe. This is pre-Covid, so this all feels very OCD, but we get it down to a fine art.

The side effects of these chemo meds are nothing compared to what he has just been through. The main issue is that they suppress his immune system right down so he is extremely vulnerable to infections, germs, bugs... Neutropenic, hardly any neutrophils. Winter is coming (and like Jon Snow, I know nothing about what it's like to have a child with leukaemia in Winter) so colds and flu viruses will abound; this will need to be carefully managed. Pandemics and Covid-19 are still in the future at this point, so sanitizer is not yet part of most people's common vocabulary. Liver function is also affected by the meds, so regular blood tests are done to monitor how his liver is coping, he may also get more tired and have any number of other side effects, but his hair will grow back, his chicken nugget weight will go back down, and he won't appear, visibly, like he has cancer.

Through the intensive phase I have frequently had weird moments where I picture myself crossing the road with the three boys after school pick-up and how we must look to everyone around us in their cars or walking out of school: toddler on my hip, little boy with giant school backpack holding onto my coat on one side, and a smaller boy with a white, bald head bobbing above his backpack grasping my other hand. Cars would always stop to let us cross. You could sometimes almost feel the type of smile the driver was giving us, "My goodness, please, cross the road, your hands are full but I see you have bigger things happening as well, please go ahead…"

Sometimes just the human smile from a granny-aged woman driving a car and waving us across could be enough to make me catch my breath: this is who we are, my god! I imagine her later on when she gets home to her husband, in a thoughtful voice,

"I saw one of the school mums crossing the road today, three little boys she had, and one of them must have been having chemotherapy for cancer, little bald head…he was a dear little thing, waved a thank you to me as I let them cross with a great big smile on his face."

"Oh yes… sad, you never know what life's going to throw at you do you," says the husband.

"There but for the grace of God I thought to myself, cancer doesn't pick and choose now does it?"

And then they might talk about the friends and family members who are battling it right now, the friend who lost their battle recently, so-and-so's cousin who detected it early… Maybe I flatter myself that it merits more than a passing pang of sympathy and shock, and actually cancer in its various nasty forms is SO everywhere that it is not so remarkable.

Either way, if Josh's appearance inadvertently etches a little mark on any hearts and thereby encourages kindness, empathy and perspective, then this will not have been an experience of meaningless suffering.

Something that happens within the first couple of

weeks of Maintenance once the initial heady, fizzing rush of passing the milestone is behind us, is what I call the 'settling'. My mum returns to the UK and I gear up mentally so I am ready to go headlong into this new, exciting, less-stressful phase, but I can't find it, I can't find that springboard to catapult me forward. I can feel my energy levels slumping, my energy is almost a tangible thing, a fine sand which I am desperately trying to cling onto and hold in my hands but I can't, it is trickling ever-faster through my fingers and I am stumbling. My wonderful psychotherapist said this would happen, she prepared me for it, I knew it was coming.

Josh meanwhile quickly settles into a hoppity-skippity central line-free high, and leaps from day to day. And whilst I am content, happy, and I recognize absolutely how exciting this is, that his oncology team were happy to sign off on the aggressive chemo phase, it dawns on me that I am absolutely exhausted. Almost immediately, Albie, now a sparky nineteen month old toddler, starts to get molars and wakes again and again through the night, every night – it's like he had put his teeth on hold while Josh was in the intensive phase so that we could all cope (which is awesome and weird in its own right). But now here they come, his gums red and white with pressure, raw with cutting edges, I am sympathetic but oh...oh for an unbroken night. Please just get them all at once in a couple of weeks and then be done! I morph into zombie-mama, deep purple shadows under my eyes, the weight of what has happened to us sinks in and combines with the sleep deprivation; I am a wreck. I stagger from day to night, minimizing conversation in the school playground at drop off, sunnies firmly down over my eyes.

The adrenalin and the cortisol hormones played their role spectacularly well I now see, carrying me through those first months; the horror of the diagnosis and the enfolding drama required an all-guns-blazing hormonal, maternal, physiological response. And now as those chemicals in my body ease off and we are no longer constantly refuelling both the damn car and our minds in order to make the next hospital appointment, logistically as well as practically, the strain of the previous months hits me hard. Tiredness doesn't come close; I look back with envy on those newborn days where you feed and burp and change and feed and burp and change basically all night for weeks and weeks on end; this is a whole new level. The newborn haze, for me, was exactly that: a haze. With first baby Ollie I found the shock of being so tired almost an additional element to the tiredness. But with the second and third babies you know that the tiredness alone won't actually kill you, you know it won't last forever, and you know there are other parents up doing the same thing no matter what time it is, or how many times you have already been up that night, you are NEVER alone. But this…

This is unreal. I am so tired mentally as well as physically, I have never know anything like it. I have always been a closet armchair-mountaineer; one of those people who reads and re-reads books about summitting Everest, K2, crossing the Poles, solo ascents of the North Face of the Eiger, my favourite movies include Alive (the football team whose plane crashed in the Andes in the 1970s) and Apollo 13, true stories about what we as humans can endure and how hard we can push ourselves. So I have read other people's descriptions of exhaustion and physical suffering. Now obviously I am not suggesting I am experiencing anything remotely approaching this (I am snorting with laughter as I write that), I'm not experiencing any physical suffering at all, quite the opposite. But there are days when I am so exhausted that the idea of walking the thirteen steps from the sitting room to the bedroom, to go to bed, is overwhelming and I seriously consider just lying down where I am on the sofa. I am not sick, I am not depressed, there is no underlying issue. I talk it through, slightly befuddled, at the start of a session with my brilliant therapist, and she rightly abandons any plans she had to untangle any specific mental knots and I just lie on her sofa with my feet up while she guides me through a meditation about being in a valley with no thought. This is what I want: no thought. For no-one to need me.

But when you have a husband and three children and one of them has leukaemia, and one is a toddler, and one is in Year 2, and your husband is away four nights each week, you don't have the option of stopping, so we just somehow keep going. I make my nest on Albie's floor more permanent and snug: a proper mattress made up with fresh linen, a giant snuggly blanket and a hot water bottle, these damn nights are going to be comfy if nothing else. As I haul myself out of bed the first time he wakes I think of all the other mums I know who are doing the same and repeat again and again in my head: you are not alone, you are not alone. The evil voice tries to interject with a, "But none of them has a son with leu- "

NO.

It won't help anything. And it won't make Josh's chances any better. Just. Keep. Going.

And after weeks and weeks, one miraculous night he only wakes three times instead of five, and then only twice instead of three, and then, oh heaven, he sleeps ALL NIGHT LONG TWICE IN A ROW.

CHAPTER 24

Day 302

A few months into Maintenance we are invited on a weekend with Camp Quality, an absolutely amazing children's cancer charity whose slogan 'laughter is the best medicine' is at the heart of all they do. Right from the first week after Josh was diagnosed we received regular emailed invitations to all sorts of uplifting events ranging from international sports matches, fun days and circus events right through to 'Mini Camps' for patients and siblings, and whole weekends away for the whole family with other families who are also going through it. While Josh has his central line and the chemo is so intensive, I read these invites wistfully with starry-eyes, wondering how we will ever get to the point where we can consider doing relatively normal fun family things like this again. The idea of being more than a couple of hours from either our Sydney hospital or our lovely local hospital at home is unfathomable; if he spikes a fever we must be within reach of Emergency departments and wards who know us.

But once Maintenance begins, I realize how important it is that we begin to tiptoe back into the normality which we hope will resume after he rings the bell in another eighteen months, if all goes well. Psychologically for me, having been by his side and entered into such a weird, abnormal world, this is a real challenge. Children adapt quickly, and even though I am someone who loves change and for the most part thrills to it, I cannot make the mental adjustment from 'crisis mode' to 'we can basically do most things now' overnight. I feel like an oil tanker; the command to change course has been given by the captain, but it is going to be a slow process to get on that new heading.

But the captain knows that the tanker will actually turn at some point, and so when a Camp Quality invite lands in my inbox for a weekend in Perisher, a ski resort in the Snowy Mountains, slap bang in the middle of the ski season, I almost faint with excitement. Scott grew up skiing with his dad and friends in the back country of the Australian mountains, later he was an instructor in the French Alps, skiing was his 'thing' for a good chunk of his 20s. Since his spinal cord injury five years ago he hasn't tested out whether he can ski. We have discussed it and found ways of feeling hopeful about his 'new physical normal', with his carbon fibre leg brace and a couple of other adjustments. He can instruct our small boys to ski and go at their pace too, he can stay on the green slopes with them, wide motorways with slow, steady turns, we can visit ski resorts in quiet seasons... This Perisher weekend sounds beyond perfect as an re-introduction for Scott back to the snow but also of course, and more importantly, for the boys. None of them has even seen proper, deep snow! They don't know the feeling of stepping into a foot of powder and seeing it puff up around your knee, or trudging through heavy snow, the crunch of the drift as it compacts beneath your boot. They have yet to stand under falling flakes with their tongues out, spinning dizzily like sweet Red-Riding-Hooded children on Swedish Christmas cards.

We are one of the lucky families, we get a spot! I jump for joy and tell the boys, they shriek with excitement, eyes glittering, and start jumping off the sofas doing their standard parkour floor-is-lava routine. Scott fizzes with glee, he fizzes so well when he is happy.

Over the next few weeks I reply to organizational emails; Camp Quality is phenomenal, every last detail is considered, and the costs are all covered so as a family you don't have to make decisions based on whether you can stretch to it, you are free to focus on whether it is physically and medically going to work for you. I absorb all this goodwill and support in quiet astonishment; this world really has so much Good in it.

Most of the snow gear is provided but we need to find helmets, goggles, gloves, the little things. We borrow it all from friends who share in our excitement and my trepidation. The mums especially get a real sense of what a big deal this is for me, our first attempt at doing something not just normal but slightly adventurous. Nights away, the whole family together, a long drive, a hotel stay, freezing weather, snow fun, and in the background a small, quavering, questioning voice in my head saying, "What if he spikes a fever? What then?" Our hospital team has the answer, concrete solid voices, mostly from our wonderful Glaswegian outreach nurse: they share his medical notes with the nearest hospital so they know what to do if things go wrong.

It sounds good, it couldn't be better, the stars are aligned. I mark the boys as absent from school, they tell their teachers who share our glee and excitement. The week running up to our departure is a big one; events at school, Albie has some broken nights, I struggle to get basic household things done before 11pm each night, and by the day before I haven't packed. I am calm, this will work out, we can leave mid-morning, I am an organizational wizard by now and it will be fine. I want to be so prepared that everything is enjoyable. I want the fire set when we leave so that when we come home on Sunday all I have to do is strike a match and warm the house. I freeze their school packed lunches so I only have to add the fresh fruit and veg on Sunday night. I lay out their school clothes ready for Monday morning. It will all be fine.

Friday morning we wake up, boys leaping on our bed, Albie shouting excitedly even though the word 'snow' is just a new word for him to practise. I make the packed lunches for the long car journey, Scott straps his kit onto the roofrack, we fill water bottles, clean out the rabbit's hutch and leave big bowls of cat biscuits around the house for Reggie (how perfect is two nights away? Short enough for pets to be fine, long enough to feel you had a break). Ollie hides cat treats in Reggie's favourite sleeping spots 'so when he misses us and curls up feeling sad he gets a nice surprise'. Josh does puzzles, Albie flits from each of us to the next eating strawberries (or as he calls them, 'sheebas'. "Mum! More! Sheebas!").

We load up, excitement mounting. A friend has lent us her very old portable DVD player which plugs into the 12V thing in the car and there is much discussion about what to watch first. About twelve DVDs make it into the car, I am secretly impressed that the bickering between the big boys still results in two Tractor Ted DVDs for little Albie. The sun is beaming, everything is gorgeous, we are off!

We cruise solidly through the beautiful Southern Highlands countryside past fields, cows, farmsteads, rolling hills, colour is everywhere. We chat excitedly and happily;

as family departures go that was a good one, Scott and I didn't have a massive fight, the boys only asked twenty-odd times how long til we could leave, Reggie the cat didn't get out at the last minute, everyone has done a wee.

Our standard going-on-a-trip procedure, not that we have done it for a while, usually involves me spending the few days in the run up making organized packing lists for each family member, doing groceries for whatever food is required for the journey, planning their outfits to travel in, locating and packing everyone's bags except Scott's, doing all the laundry so we don't come back to chaos, emptying the fridge of stuff that will go mouldy, making a mental note of what's in the freezer for dinner when we get home, organizing the pets, and then on the day assembling the food, filling water bottles, wiping down surfaces, closing certain shutters and leaving some open (Hello robbers! We are not really away!), checking all the various bikes, trucks and diggers are under cover, pouring loo cleaner in the loos after everyone has done a wee, taking all the luggage to the carport so Scott can pack the boot Tetris-style, and handing out snacks to stem the tide of, "How long til we can gooooooo?!"

Scott, during this time of intense activity, is likely to be found clipping his toenails on his own in a quiet corner before picking up his bag, putting it in the car and then saying with an air of impatience, "Right, come on, what's taking so long?! Let's go!" He is then highly likely to strap all three boys into their seats and start the engine so they get really excited, leaving me to get them out again to do grumpy last minute wees to a chorus of, "Eurgh Mu-u-um why can't we just gooooooo?" Mum is so annoying. Dad is so fun how he just wants to go on holiday!

But amazingly enough that didn't happen this time. Maybe our inflicted bigger-picture perspective means our excitement and appreciation for what we are about to do is shielding us from annoyance. How poetic. Or maybe Scott's toenails are for some reason just not a priority for this trip.

We barrel along in the sunshine. Ten minutes in the boys ask for crisps; I had bought a massive bag as a special holiday treat, we don't normally have crisps in the house hence their massive post-GA appeal in the recovery days. Sour Cream & Chives, cheap wiggly ones, delicious. We ration them until we get to the 'fast road', and true to form as we glide to merge onto the highway Josh sticks his arm through the middle of the car and asks in his little-boy voice for 'lots and lots please'. I acquiesce, even Albie gets some and holds them up in amazed delight saying, "Wow!? Wow!?" Everyone crunches contentedly.

"Mum I have a tummy ache," Josh's voice, sounding a bit flat. I sigh inwardly – he only had a kiwifruit for breakfast so the crisps are probably not ideal - and make a mental list of what stomach-settling sustenance I packed in the bag at my feet. None of them has ever been car sick so vomiting doesn't really cross my mind.

"Oh dear darling that's not good, we still have about 4 hours in the car to go, maybe some water?"

"No. More crisps might help."

He sounds quiet. I grab another handful and turn around to give him a bolstering smile and deliver them straight into his little cupped hands.

Oh no. His little round face is white, all one colour. He looks freezing cold.

"Josh, are you cold?"

He is sitting on the sunny side of the car, he should be overheating and flushed if anything.

"A bit." He shivers.

My brain hits the pause button, Scott feels it. Houston, we (may) have a problem. The thermometer is usually in my handbag but I have switched to a backpack for this snowy weekend so everything has been rearranged and is in the wrong place. The thermometer is in his medicine bag with all his chemo tablets, and that is packed in the car boot.

I run through the list of what might make him perk up, offering him various options. He doesn't feel nauseous, he says he isn't going to be sick. He eats a couple more crisps.

Even though he is probably just feeling a bit weird we can't take any chances, there is a service station in 1km and we pull in. Scott tops up with diesel while I get the thermometer from the boot and wait the now-familiar precise thirty-seven seconds for it to read his temperature.
38.1
EVERY SWEARWORD. NO WAY. You are KIDDING me. I close the car door and walk round to the other side where Scott is filling the tank.

"Take a deep breath," I give him a second or two to register. I hold out the thermometer. 38.1

Our faces fall, our chests thud. We don't look at each other. Surely not.

"Take it again," he says, "just in case."

And like every other about-to-be-disappointed cancer mum before me, I take it again, hoping and hoping that it will have plummeted a full 1.7 degrees to his customary 36.4 and we can put it down to a faulty thermometer. Like hell, as if hospital-issued thermometers are ever faulty.

37.9 Hmm.

Scott pays for the fuel and we get back in, silent, tense. There is no option to turn around at this service station so Scott continues to the next exit. We start to talk it through, trying desperately not to be too blatant in our word choices so the boys don't realize immediately.

The protocol states that 38 degrees or higher means 48 hours in hospital on iv antibiotics. He is in Maintenance so we don't have to rush to Emergency quite as fast as when he had a central line, but we can't hang around. On the other hand 37.9 is not 38. But it was 38.1. I pass Josh the thermometer and get him to take it again.

38.1

If we keep going, we are driving further and further away from 'our' hospitals, if he gets hotter while we are there he will have to go into a new different hospital which will all be unfamiliar and he will be scared, I will have to explain everything to everyone, and then we will be stuck there with the other boys for at least forty-eight hours. Apart from any of that, we are going on a Camp Quality weekend for goodness sake, we will be among immuno-suppressed children like Josh, we can't possibly risk passing anything on to them. Scott and I claw at ideas, desperately searching for a lifeline, I feel like we are hanging off a grassy cliff and the grass and mud is slipping through our fingers, we have no option but to let go, we have to give in to gravity and fall down off the cliff, gravity is obvious, a rule of science, a law. And 38 degrees is the law of our world.

And there is another whole layer of worry: this past week there have been two cases of chicken pox at his school and we have been doing our utmost to avoid exposure. Chicken pox can be fatal for children on chemo, as can measles. The child with chicken pox came into the playground to pick up the other sibling, teachers took Josh out of different doors to avoid walking past them, my blood pressure sky-rocketed and then settled, sky-rocketed and then settled… Countless phonecalls with our long-suffering Glaswegian nurse who risks annoyance by checking again and again with the oncology god. If he is definitely and directly exposed to the virus he will need something nicknamed 'the zig' which basically sounds like a whopper of an injection followed by several hours of observation (it is a blood product, which means there is a small risk of a reaction such as anaphylaxis or a temperature spike), but they don't want him to miss school just on the offchance that he happens to encounter an infected child. The oncology god defines 'exposure' in minute detail for me. The definition of exposure differs from child to child depending on their own resistance to the virus. Josh is strong; they feel it is likely he has managed to retain some of his immunity to the virus from before he developed leukaemia (chemo can erase the protection that vaccines provide – I'm sure that's not the medical way to describe it but that is the end effect). Josh had full-blown, spectacular chicken pox as a baby when he was too young to have been immunised, and then was fully vaccinated for everything under the sun so was, prior to leukaemia, as protected as he could have been when he started treatment.

And our particular oncology god rightly places immense importance on school attendance and the child feeling as normal as possible: the negative impacts of keeping them away from school out of fear of possible exposure to viruses have to be weighed up against the actual risk. It's a weird one; the risk if he contracted chicken pox is very serious, life-threatening. But the chance is pretty remote. 'Pretty remote'. The right language doesn't exist to sum up the gravity and yet the perspective you have to somehow harness. Imagine queueing for a ride at a theme park and sitting in the seat, clunking down the safety barrier and the attendant saying, "Yeah there's a chance it will pop up and you'll plummet to your death but it's pretty remote." Hmm.

So. Back to our car journey. All this whirls around my head, and Scott's, as we drive through the beautiful sunny day. We know what we have to do, it is just taking time to sink in. We don't have the luxury of being oil tankers now though, we need to be the Manly Jetcat, powerful jets blasting us decisively in a new direction. He takes the exit, we drive over the highway and back down the ramp to join it in the opposite direction.

Ollie notices, big eyes, "Mum, why are we going back?!"

I take a deep breath and look at Scott. He says, "Mum and I need to explain something." Josh wells up immediately, "Am I hot? Do I have to go to hospital? Are we not going to the snow?"

"Boys," I begin, I am welling up and sniffing, "Very sadly Joshie has a fever and we are going to have to turn around and go back home."

Their faces absolutely break and go red, both look out of their respective windows and big fat tears pour down their cheeks instantly. Neither of them shouts or is angry or noisy at all.

I continue, "I am so sorry we have to change our plan. I know this is so sad and we are all incredibly disappointed but we have to look after Josh." I am also crying now.

Albie looks fascinated, kicks his legs in his car seat and yells in philosophical excitement, "Mummy! Sad! CRY!?!"

The car feels too-bright with dazzling, desperate, panicked disappointment. I reach back and grab Ollie's hand hard and he squeezes it again and again, I love you I love you, as he cries and cries quietly. I am so f*cking angry with the universe it is all I can do not to roar and scream.

Then Ollie cries out as though grasping at a final hope, "What about the DVD player? We were going to watch DVDs!"

We can still do that.

I locate the DVD player and fumble clumsily to get the wire into the 12V car thing. I press the ON switch.

Nothing happens. I turn it over, ah, I haven't plugged the wire into the machine. I get a vague sense through the fog of my raging disappointment that this might make quite a funny story one day. I stuff the jack into the hole on the side of the machine, it doesn't seem to want to stay in, but my friend told me they would wedge it as hard as they could between the car seats, she was pretty clear they weren't precious about it and had said several times that it might not work.

"Now remember boys it might not work…"

A tearful debate ensues: "I want to watch Inside Out!"

"No I want The Incredibles!"

"How about something Albie – "

I can smell smoke, I can smell an electrical fire.

"Scott I can smell an electrical fire I can smell oh my god there is smoke coming out of the Scott there is smoke there is smoke…"

Smoke starts billowing slowly out of the portable DVD player, it smells awful, I yank the wire out of the 12V thing and out of the player. I peer into the 12V hole, nothing exciting happening in there, the smoke continues, what the hell is happening, we are already only just functioning dealing with the disappointment of driving the wrong way, what the hell, how fast can I think, this is insane. I hold it out in front of me turning it checking it for actual real live flames. No flames, just smoke. He is driving in the fast lane, there is traffic in the slow lane, he can't pull over.

My voice is level but panicked, "Pull over, what do I, this is – "

"I can't pull over here I know I know it's smoking."

We are talking to each other like weird kind of R2D2s.

"My finger is on the window I am about to throw it out of the window shall I throw it out of the window is it going to explode?"

"Is it still smoking I·can't look I am driving?"

"It's stopping no it's still going no I think it's stopping oh god pull over no it's stopping it's ok I think."

It actually doesn't feel very hot.

"What is it Scott why is it smoking?"

"It's an electrical fire inside there must be dust it must have short circuited and burnt dust somewhere it's because this car is always so filthy."

Erm? WTF?

I will not be drawn on this, the car actually is filthy right now, there is probably enough stale food in and around the various car seats and boosters and floor mats to feed a small family of possums. I had vaguely considered vacuuming it before we went to Perisher, then remembered I barely had time to hang out the laundry this week, let alone the energy, and then realized it would only get filthier during the roadtrip anyway, and shoved that ridiculous idea aside. Anyway, I am not sure that the relative filth of the school run could be justifiably blamed for starting an electrical fire in my friend's DVD player.

It has stopped smoking. A tiny part of me is very faintly disappointed that I didn't get to throw it out of the window and I know my friend would be equally disappointed, she is the most down to earth person I know and I feel confident that she would find the image of me hurling a smoking 1990s portable device out of a moving car on the Hume Highway absolutely superb. Although this way at least I won't have the guilt of having polluted the poor planet by chucking some completely non-degradable plastic into the bushes. (It dawns on me now that this is of course Australia and we are in the middle of a serious drought, so had it actually been in flames it could have started a horrific bushfire within seconds. Note to self: always hurl smoking devices onto the hard shoulder, NOT into the bush.)

We are close to home now. Scott and I are quiet, wide-eyed and probably slightly in mild shock at the amount our brains are computing right now.

Ollie announces, "Well I AM very disappointed that we are not going to Perisher but at least we are all alive and not burning in a fire from the DVD player!"

Yes, he is right. Nice one Ollie. The blissful simplicity of the seven year old switching from emotion to emotion. Actually, nice one DVD player and dear friend who leant it to us, thank you for the much-needed perspective.

As we drive the final kilometer towards home I pass Joshie the thermometer: 38.4. We are doing the right thing. We pull up, we are not panicking, Scott starts unstrapping the roofrack, Ollie unloads the boot, Albie is thrilled and stomps around shouting, "Home! Home!" Reggie the cat looks at us in confusion: why did you go out for an hour and leave me so many biscuits, humans?

Josh steps out of the car, shouts, "MUM!" and promptly vomits all over the front porch. Undigested crisps and water, he is surprised and horrified and I rush to hold his shoulders as his little body convulses again and again getting every last damn crisp out. You're ok, you're ok. He continues spitting the last bits out on the front lawn. I wipe him down and he perches on the front step as I go into mental overdrive: what do we need, Redkite bag, is it missing anything, grab his meds, I am wearing furry snowboots...

As I run, literally, from car to house grabbing various things I dial first our Glaswegian to update her, she is steady, calm, sympathetic, functional, perfect. Then the local children's ward to alert them that we are coming in, they are great and confirm we should go straight to them and bypass Emergency. They give me the heads up that there is a brand new lovely Registrar on rotation so I can prepare Josh. This is a bonus as I can remind him again that the poor original one who had to try to do his cannula three times on that first awful day is long gone.

And then the saddest call, while I am pulling on my normal shoes, to Camp Quality. I dial the lovely lady in charge and my throat closes up, my voice breaks, I tell her what happened and how horribly disappointed we all are. She immediately gets it and said she had just put the phone down to another mum who was also crying as the same thing had happened to their little girl. This stops me in my sniveling tracks: we really are never alone. I start apologizing profusely, so much organization and cost on their part, it's all funded by the generosity of the public donations, fundraising, so much effort and so last minute, and she interrupts and reminds me gently that this is their world, they are a children's cancer charity, this happens, and frequently. She is a genius, she seems to know how to say the kind words I need to hear but without being so kind and empathetic that I dissolve into a complete wreck. She knows I need to keep functioning now and get him to hospital, she knows the drill. She has either been there, or she has years of experience with cancer parents. Probably both. My respect for Camp Quality notches up even higher.

And so we hug Ollie and Albie and Daddy goodbye and set off to the hospital. I am back in practical mode now, doing what we have to do, getting Josh through it. As we walk in I wrap my gratitude cloak around me, these people are going to sort things out. I smell the familiar clean hospital smell and the disappointment momentarily rises in my throat. I pause outside the children's ward and pretend to be busy squirting antibacterial stuff on my hands while centring myself and remember to accept that this is just how it is. There is no other way of putting it, this is now.

Josh is very quiet. He knows that now he doesn't have a central line he will have to have a cannula put in. He comments to me wistfully in a tiny voice (and surprisingly drily for a little six year old) that now that his central line with its dangly easy-connect tubes is gone 'we are doing needles not noodles'.

We tell the story of what we were doing when he spiked and they set us up in our room quietly and calmly, sharing his sadness, respecting his feelings and not trying to jolly him up or convince him it's all fine. He climbs up onto his bed, there's no-one else on the ward and it is calm and peaceful, this is one of the lovely things about our local hospital. We are in our own room, a rhododendron bush has grown since we were last here and now it brushes up against our window, the friendly magnolia tree is about to explode into bloom in the courtyard outside, the sun shines. Winter in Australia.

The new, slightly disconcertingly-beautiful doctor gets the cannula in on the first attempt. I want to ask her where her stripy dress is from but feel this might be considered a bit trivial given that she has only just met us and My Son Has Leukaemia. Josh is silent while the needle pokes around trying to find the right spot in the vein, his eyes well up and he goes very red but true to form he doesn't say anything or make a noise. Our favourite nurses stick teddy bear stickers over it to hold the needle in place and his wrist is strapped onto a surfboard ("You have arrested my arm!") and hidden under a 'sock' so he doesn't have to see the spike going into his skin.

We all stand back in relief. And then as we all make general Mother Hen congratulatory noises to him for being so brave it dawns on all of us at the same time that we have put it in his right hand and he is right-handed, has at least forty-eight hours in hospital ahead of him, and was about to start doing some colouring in. I am a real live facepalm emoji. There's no way we can take it out and put in another one, we will cope. But it's a sharp, grim-faced reminder from the evil cancer gods: it doesn't matter how far through this journey you go or how many times you tell yourself You've Got This, you are still a total rookie.

He stays in for the required forty-eight hours of iv antibiotics and then just before we are about to leave we notice a rash 'blossoming' on his ankles and hands. My stomach lurches sickeningly; chicken pox and measles please no. Pretty remote. Can be fatal. That hideous, brutally final word.

We wait with our two nurse-angels for the paediatrician to arrive (it is Sunday morning and we are the only people on the ward) and try not to overanalyze the rash. It doesn't look measly right now. Separate dots in specific areas. And Josh is well, I am not sitting next to a child who looks or seems in any way like someone developing a potentially fatal illness. I realize I have become hardened now, I am very good at shutting down the evil voice in my head with its insidious 'what if…' suggestions; no, you will not affect me, I am immune to you now. After I have sat next to my child being suffused with powerful neon-coloured chemo hour after hour, week after week, watched him expand so much that he can barely see out of his eyelids and then shrink back down to a little skinny bean, brushed the hairs off his pillow each morning and then watched the fuzz tentatively reappear, twice, no you evil little voice, I am stronger than you and I can shut you down now. I cannot spare the energy on worry, I need every bit of it to function.

I hear the doctor's voice in the corridor and the nurses brief him at high speed, he sweeps in, takes one look and declares, "Nope, not varicella!" He takes a swab from one of the open sores, reels off a few virus names I recognize but isn't overly concerned, and I realize how bizarre, and also reassuring, it is to find yourself in a hospital setting for essentially a GP-level illness. This feels, in an odd way, a perverse luxury to me; any qualms or worries that I have can be referred to specialists whose numbers are stored in my phone.

We can go home, everyone is calm, the rash will develop and do its thing and we can come back in the morning for a review, and of course again and again I am told if anything changes come straight back, phone us first… The care and attention is superlative. Once again I am struck by how much our medical team appears to consider the wider family; they know they could keep Josh in to observe how the rash develops, but they also know that he is more comfortable mentally and physically at home, and he is the middle one of three boys, all of whom need their mummy. The more we can find a semblance of normality the better. So home we go.

The rash does develop, but in a boring way, and inevitably Josh passes the virus on to Albie, but we are calm, we've got this now. Two doses of paracetamol for Albie and his rash develops, I am serene. It is absolutely one hundred per cent down to the safety net I can almost feel surrounding us; we are plodding on but if we wobble, if anyone wobbles, we are five minutes from help. The gratitude is like a big jelly sitting all over us, I am a human terrine.

The following day we get a name for our virus: enterovirus. This doesn't change anything we have been told or anything we have to do next, so I don't bother googling, don't want to know. It takes weeks for the dots to fade completely, and as an extra kick in the teeth, Josh's fingernails start lifting off. Some of the dots were beneath his nails on the pink nailbed, and now those dots don't seem to be able to fade away without pushing the nails off first. My little six year old, this is just so damn unfair. He bobs off to school each morning waving merrily through the schoolgates with little white band-aids wrapped around his fingertips, coming home with them all filthy from lead pencils and ball games and scratching around in the sandpit at lunchtime…

He isn't that bothered; he says his nails don't hurt, it's just annoying being scared that they will rip off before they are ready to fall off. He's more interested in seeing how slowly the new nails grow underneath the old ones, "because before the world was divided into different continents did you know Mum that 300 million years ago it was all one big, big land called Pangaea, and then it broke up and separated and the pieces of land moved apart AT THE SAME SPEED THAT NAILS GROW?!! So now we can see how fast the land moved!" Way to get a perspective on your own troubles little man.

THE GRATITUDE CLOAK

CHAPTER 25

Day 439

As it continues, I find Maintenance very, very weird. I talk at length to my psychotherapist about it, describing the way that I bob along and life feels really quite normal: Ollie and Josh argue and bicker, then flash in the blink of an eye to huge-hearted hugs and engulfing love, there is wee on the loo seat, you stress about what to have for dinner, Ollie does a kitten voice ALL AFTERNOON, you put more laundry on, hang it out, cuddle someone who has bumped their head, do you need the frozen peas, ok eat some frozen peas instead (always works), for the fifth time PYJAMAS, TEETH AND WEE... and then several times each day this thud punches you in the stomach: oh yes, cancer. He doesn't look or seem sick any more. But medically he is nowhere near ringing the bell yet. More than a year of oral chemo to go, and that's if all goes well. Somehow I have to find a way to keep swimming, just keep swimming, Keep Calm and Carry On. I worry I am becoming completely and utterly disconnected from my feelings, am I faking it? Does it matter if I am? I don't think I am, I feel honest with the reality we are living in, and yet the thud always stops me in my tracks.

Together with my psychotherapist I work out that I have to view the thud from a different perspective. If I can convert it in my mind into a reminder to slow down and do something for me, find my Hygge again, then maybe I can accept it, maybe even embrace it. Instead of living in fear of the reminder that my son is fighting leukaemia, over and over again, I need to acknowledge that fear, yes I am afraid, and just walk alongside it and accept it for what it is: a fully justified emotion in response to a properly frightening scenario which is not going to change for months and months. Because that's all it is. Tackling it head on with indignant aggression or trying to resist it, battling it day after day, would be exhausting and deeply unpleasant. If I imagine turning so I'm next to it, the fear, then we walk together, forwards. It takes me a while to do this, it's not the walking partner I'd choose, but the more I am aware of this idea the more easily I find I can put it into action. Oh hi, you again, come on, walk with me. Breathe and move forwards.

I begin to try to live my own life with the fundamental mantra that worry is pointless: worry doesn't take away tomorrow's troubles, it steals today's peace. I step outside and look up to the sky, the tops of the gumtrees, drought-blasted in this ominous Australian time of climate change. The branches sway one hundred feet up, stringy bark straggles its way down the trunk. The trees don't worry, they just drop a branch when they're under stress, shed some weight. They take decisive action to ensure they have less to manage and less to care for. As I internalize this new distancing from worry and anxiety I feel a strange, quiet, strong sense of freedom coming over me, maybe, just maybe, I am starting on the path towards achieving that nirvana of living in the now, in the moment. The Danes know it, this is Hygge again in a different form. I look down at little Albie, grounded far below the tree tops, two years old, busily and proudly weeing into a hole in the garden path with his tiny, squidgy bare bottom out and his bright yellow wellies, totally focused on how wonderful it is to be able to steer your wee; he is the master of living right now, this is what I need to channel. Not the weeing with my bum out, but the now-ness. Camp Quality, the wonderful charity, call it Kidness.

As more time passes and Josh is still in Maintenance, we begin to look completely normal. We are regularly at school, the boys start Years 1 and 3 and I continue to take the older boys into the playground. I get into the habit of swirling my gratitude cloak around me and walking in with a very normal smile, chat to friends. Josh's hair grows back and he has actual haircuts. I will never be blasé about haircuts again; I marvel at it as it falls onto the hair salon floor, or flies away in the wind when we do garden haircuts with the kitchen scissors... I like to think of birds using it to make their nests snug, blissfully ignorant of the horrors that this hair came back from.

But we still have months and months and months of chemo and treatment ahead, it is not over. A friend texts me to say it must be so nice to get back to normality. I know exactly what she means, and it is nice as she says, but part of me also wants to reply in wailing, sobbing capital letters: IT'S NOT NORMAL! HE'S STILL ON CHEMO! NOTHING IS BETTER! HE'S NOT CURED! But of course I can't. I send a heart emoji, I don't want to seem churlish. Her message comes from kindness.

Ollie begs to take the bus to and from school with his friends and I would dearly love to say yes; the idea of not having to face the playground full of people-who-are-not-cancer-mums twice a day for drop off and pick up is so appealing I almost want to weep, but Josh has a severely compromised immune system so the bus is basically just another place to pick up germs and bring them home to Josh. School is enough of a petri dish.

I also need to channel the gum tree and their habit of dropping a branch if it rains and they get too waterlogged, or if there is a drought and they are starved of hydration. Some friendships and relationships begin to feel like very heavy branches which are adding to my mental load. My own father has been silent for over a year now, not a card to Josh, nothing at Christmas, nothing at birthdays, just a characteristically dysfunctional silence. He lives on the other side of the planet, and had sent a peculiar email when Josh was diagnosed saying how wonderful it must be for us to know Josh was going to be absolutely fine. It read like a passive-aggressive suggestion that I was over-reacting and sensationalizing everything. After that, deafening silence. A dedicated therapy session with my 24 carat gold psychotherapist helps me decide that the time has come to stop even thinking of him, stop wondering why he is silent. It is not my story. I drop this waterlogged branch. To my delight, I feel nothing, not even relief. And it isn't a suppressed 'nothing', it's a genuine 'this has been worked through, he brings nothing positive to me or my children, I am good without him'. Blood pressure stays level.

Similarly, while most friendships have been bolstering and incredibly supportive all the way through, one in particular has become overpowering; the insistence on dramatizing every detail and assumptions of how I must be feeling, telling me what I must need by way of support, that I really should be sitting down more often to talk through everything and sob, begins to cause an actual headache. I don't feel like sobbing all the time, and I don't like being made to feel that I should be. It is adding another layer of negativity to my already-fried brain; I find myself replaying conversations wishing I had been stronger, clearer, more assertive instead of humming and ahhing and nodding along. I am a total pushover, and I don't like how it makes me feel about myself. This is a deeply uncomfortable one for me to get my head around; I am not ungrateful for the support, every word and action comes from a place of kind intentions, and yet it boils down to the simple fact that I do not live in a state of drama and I emphatically do not want to be exposed to drama just because someone else's response to what I am going through would be dramatic. At times it almost feels as though the kindness is motivated slightly by a lust for the sensational, an irresistible urge to know the latest gossip, salacious or not. A pushiness. And for a car crash, a one-off crisis moment then maybe this is absolutely fine, but we still have months and months to go on our path towards that Bell in the oncology clinic, I don't want my own experience of this rich, challenging, beautiful, precious life being reflected back at me through the super-dramatic lens of someone else's response to it.

And there's plenty to get dramatic about, since life keeps throwing us curveballs, holy moley…

Some, but not all, of the curveballs involve Josh: four months into Maintenance his liver throws a hissy fit, decides it's had enough chemo and starts going mental. The numbers on the tests skyrocket and plummet and stabilise and spike again, it's as though his liver is going on its own private rollercoaster ride over and over again. For weeks his dosages are tweaked, process of elimination is employed, different tactics are used, full blood counts and liver function tests (just a regular blood test but with more tickboxes) happen frequently, the oncology god rubs his chin and confers with his fellow gods. They confer and they concur. Time ticks on.

Other curveballs involve Scott: six months into Maintenance he just shuts down and fades out, there is no other way to describe it. He is numb, nothing registers any more, he has slowed to sloth-pace, sleeps forty-six hours straight two weekends running, it has all become too much. I manage to drag him to the GP who takes one look, identifies this as a severe depressive episode and knows what to do (this woman, this wonderful woman, I have yet to work out how we express our gratitude to her when we come out of the other side of whatever we are in). He is built back up, clambering out of the trough while I watch and wait, frequently gnashing my teeth in desperation, frustration, rage, hopelessness, but for the most part trying so, so hard to epitomize my star sign Taurus: 'stubborn, determined, loyal' (I remember a little horoscope book I was given age ten and how I pored over the different star signs and their traits, who would marry whom, what their life held in store…the three words have always stuck with me). I wish my husband, my friend, would return so much it hurts my stomach.

And more curveballs when our other boys get sick: Albie has viral-induced wheeze for the first time and after Josh's experience I am so focused on his fever that I don't even notice him wheezing. The mum guilt that follows when the GP hands us the prescription for ventolin makes me well up. Ollie's curveballs are for the most part less exciting; his girlfriends tease him for having ham sandwiches because – durr! – ham is slices of a pig's bum and bums are gross! Or he is late for band practice and I am a bad mummy… Yes, we are a regular family with regular family issues quite apart from the leukaemia, and family life with three boys in times of economic stress isn't boring; this is us, this is our Now, we keep going.

It slowly dawns on me that having relentless heavy

chats pushed on me by 'friends' analyzing each curve in my trajectory is making things worse; it starts to feel like dead weight. The psychotherapist and GP are unequivocal: shed them, drop the branch. Do not risk your own mental health. It is a slow process and I don't feel brave; they have to help me find the words to use, with gratitude, kindness and clarity, and I have to keep reminding myself that I am forty-one and am, on paper at least, an adult.

Of course it still goes down like a cup of cold sick, thrown back at me dramatically and I am gaslit, told I am a terrible person in an eye-wateringly cruel response calculated to cause maximum hurt. The psychotherapist snorts and points out that the response confirms I was right to draw a line. I think of a podcast I listened to where Brené Brown tells Oprah Winfrey how she had to put up a boundary with a friend, and Oprah asks calmly how it was received. The response was along the lines of, "Oh she went batshit crazy!" It's ok, batshit crazy happened to the mighty Brené too. To paraphrase some of her best advice, choose temporary discomfort over resentment.

So my waterlogged branches drop, I begin to feel leaner, lighter.

THE GRATITUDE CLOAK

CHAPTER 26

18 months in – Day 579

Three quarters of the way through, and Josh has an over-active weekend, catches a cold and is admitted to hospital at 38.4. It feels awful initially as I meet Josh's eyes after taking his temperature, his wide-eyed, "Do we have to go in?" in a resigned tone heavy with 'I remember this'… The lump in both our throats wins and we hug and cry into each other's necks while helpless Scott and white-faced Ollie watch, yes darling we have to go in (SWEARWORD SWEARWORD SWEARWORD as I GNASH my teeth this is NOT OK for this little person). I stamp on my inner voice and off we go. Once there, we click straight into the routine and the crisis moment passes astonishingly fast; this is the clearest ever demonstration of how hardened we have become, how we have adapted. Instead of forty-eight hours of shock, we have ten minutes of resignation and then we are in the zone. Our biggest stress, once we are in the car and on the way, is that the Redkite hospital bag, which has by now travelled thousands of kilometres with us in the boot in the past year and a half (hundreds of school runs, hundreds of up and downs to Sydney, to playgroup, the supermarket, always ready just in case) is full of Summer stuff, and as of last week it is definitely Autumn and chilly. The cannula is done without so much as a raised eyebrow (trainee nurses gawp and look a bit disconcerted at his lack of interest in the needle), the meds and fluids bags go up on the pole, I set up my armchair bed and help myself from the ward linen cupboard to my requisite extra two blankets, extra pillow to fill the gap next to the wall, rolled up cellular blanket to stuff down the sides of the hinges of the bed so it doesn't scrape my legs in the night, extra towel to fold up and use as a bath mat... This is us.

But it turns out we are still humans after all. The hours tick by, day into night into day into night, and then on the third morning in hospital a friend calls straight after school assembly to say that Josh won the lucky dip. Every week the whole school's good behavior awards are all put in a big box and one name is pulled out per yeargroup – the more awards you get the higher the chance of your name being pulled out. This is a new initiative to encourage kindness, camaraderie and, obviously, consistent good behavior. Huge excitement greets the box at the end of each week's assembly, you can almost feel the hope hanging in the air above six hundred students. If your name gets pulled out you can choose a small present from a big box of cool stuff. Matchbox cars, unicorn erasers, notepads, pencils... And so my friend describes how Josh's name is pulled out and his whole class had all yelled out in explosive excitement, "He's not here! He's not here!" and soon most of the school joins in with gleeful shouts, "He's NOT HERE!" The Deputy Head restores calm and assures everyone that Josh can choose a treat when he returns to school. I laugh on the phone with my friend as she describes the merry drama, the gorgeous primary-school-age lack of cynicism, the empathetic excitement for their friend, their buddy, will they pick someone else instead, could it be me next time?

And then I hang up and it suddenly wells up like a tsunami, this feeling bubbling up from my stomach to my face and tears pour down my cheeks, it's a sweet story but I don't want Josh to be 'not here', I don't want him to be known to the whole school, dammit I don't want him to be in hospital! Still the vestiges of the earliest days are there, ready to blindside me at strange moments. There is no escaping it; I can learn to walk with the fear of him dying, I can get up and do your hair and put mascara on and smile at everyone at the school gate, I can meditate to reset my self, I can feel thankful for the 24 carat gold good stuff and turn my head to the sunshine so the shadows fall behind me, I can find stars in the darkness, rainbows in the rain, I really can now, but none of that means I stop wishing against wish against wish that this wasn't damn well happening. None of that changes the fact that it is not ok that kids get cancer.

Josh announces he wants to beat me at chess, I snap out of my self-absorbed pity-fest; he isn't crying, he wants to play chess. I tell him he won the lucky dip at assembly and he punches the air with a triumphant, "Yesssssss!!!" Live in the moment my brown-eyed boy, live in the moment.

Birthdays are interesting. He turns seven. When your child has cancer and presents you with a list of who they want to invite for a birthday playdate in the garden, it is very hard to say they have to limit it. And this is how we end up with forty-one children. Maybe no pass the parcel this year. We tie what feels like a thousand donuts on strings hanging from the rotating washing line and they race to eat them with their hands behind their backs, Mum (back from the UK for a birthday visit) sets up an ice cream stall and swiftly gets through three mega boxes of

Neapolitan and cone after cone after cone, here are your sprinkles, would you like some chocolate sauce squirted on it too? It is utter mayhem, Josh loves it, and for me it is tinged with an icy shard of 'please, please let him have lots more birthdays'. Let this not be one of the last.

At this point we have three months to go until we reach the two year mark since everything began. Through maintenance, as his liver continues to hate chemo, it has been very hard to achieve the right level of suppression without potentially damaging his liver irreparably.

The weekly blood tests look at a myriad of things to track what is going on. Josh is cool as a cucumber about this; often I take all three boys and we get it done on the way to school. Albie (now two and a half) climbs on the swivel chair and asks for stickers, Ollie pretends to eat the cotton wool balls like Will Ferrell in Elf, Josh helps lovely Kate our favourite pathologist find his favourite vein... I laugh along, half of me with my head in my hands (mentally), half of me doing the jolly mum thing, always using the boys as the 'screen'.

The end of treatment bone marrow aspirate under GA is now looming like a grim slow motion tidal wave; thanks to the liver's sensitivity, this BMA will be more nerve racking than originally thought - less of a check that it is all still ok, and more of a 'has the treatment worked'. The really detailed result, the Minimal Residual Disease analysis, can take a couple of weeks to come through. My psychotherapist, who has by now become a bit like a human lighthouse, helping me navigate this wild, dark, still-beautiful ocean without crashing into the rocks, now helps me prepare for that two week wait. The mantra is consistent: right now, we live today.

THE GRATITUDE CLOAK

CHAPTER 27

Day 727

Right here we go. Final BMA time. The night before, Josh lies in his bed seemingly fine, happily rapping the Gruffalo next to me in a Sarf London accent, inspired by that youtube dad who raps kids' books. Unlike Josh, I am a mess! As we packed our bag earlier in the day, I could feel every minute of two years creeping up and sitting quietly on my shoulders. Welcome them to my shoulders, sit with them, embrace them, this is your reality...

I am bedecked like a freaking Christmas tree: courage necklace, angel wing earrings, steel 'you've got this' bangle, a cluster of my cousins' lucky silver charms, little rose quartz guardian angel and much more. Everything is symbolic, each talisman imbued with meaning, any port in a storm, find comfort wherever I can. The day unfolds, progresses in the usual GA way, punctuated by salt and vinegar crisps and high fives. And now we wait.

Back home, school, we wait, cooking, brothers, laundry, more food please, bike riding, we wait, groceries, sunshine, notice the collateral beauty, school, husband, we wait, blossom blows off trees in the wind, dentist, school, rain, we wait, food, cooking, school, supermarket, laundry, bike riding, we wait, tick tick tick. Josh asks twice and then seems to forget about it.

Day 9: No Caller ID flashes on my phone. I'm sitting at my desk (I have a tiny, brand new, part time job two days a week, it's a holiday from everything, people ask me as they pass how I'm coping being new and in such a busy environment – I tell them with a slightly manic grin that I have three small boys at home and these two days are like a spa break. No need to overshare!)

So to No Caller ID.

"Hello?"

"Ah yes hello this is (the oncology god)." He wastes no time, doesn't draw breath - "I'm calling with excellent news, we have the results of the Minimal Residual Disease analysis and I can tell you that no leukaemia cells were able to be detected, this is exactly the result we were aiming for…" As the words register, with no 'but' or 'however' forthcoming, his voice, his calming, authoritative, serious voice starts to go into slow motion fluffballs in my brain, excellent news, excellent news, excellent news, it crescendos and breaks like a wave in my brain HE'S CLEAR!!!!! HE'S CLEAR!!!!!

I stutter out a breathless, "Oh wow…" and then as he talks about next steps, the ongoing bloods and checks and every few weeks this test and then that test, I say mmm and great and right and then keep trying to find a pause in his talking to squeeze in thank you oh thank you, thank you, yes, ok, yep, mm. I zoom up out of my body and look down on myself, observing my responses to this momentous, momentous, life-milestone moment and note that I am perfectly book-ending the two years from the first phonecall, it appears the English person has not been erased by the trauma of these past two years, I'm politely saying, "Right," a lot. Good Lord I may well get a nice cup of tea when I get off the phone. This momentous conversation ends. I try to process. I can picture the oncology god ticking Josh's name off his call list, good, done, onto the next... I don't cry or scream, I don't hold back tears. I feel it in my stomach, it's a very low down warmth, a barely-detectable but still insistent bubbling, a real reaction, it's going to stay like that for a while. Joy-relief-gratitude. I grit my teeth together and squeeze up my eyes and grin so wide my face might split and do a little happy ant dance all on my own in the office and fizz, FIZZ with gleeeeeee. I need to tell Scott, but I can't break this news to him on the phone, I need to be there in person, face to face. I have no idea how I get through the next hour or so of work, no memory at all, and then the second the clock ticks to home time I am out of the door and marching across the playing fields in the afternoon sun, a beeline to the front gate, in, and, "Scott! Scott!" He appears, his usual steady, unhurried self, a mildly curious expression on his face.

"I had a call from (the oncology god) with the results." His face is suddenly a frozen mask, inert, expectant, on the brink of explosion, not knowing whether this will be destruction or ecstasy. I tell him, "He's clear!" and it is as though the heavens around him collapse, he inhales, it seems, all the air in the garden and staggers into the middle of the front lawn, knees moving faster than his upper body despite his leg brace, and then chest out, heart to the heavens he whoop-roars, whoop-roars, whoop-roars with his arms in a dual, eternal fist-punch to the skies, yes! Yes! Yes! Not for him the gleeful happy ant dance, he is triumph personified. We stand unsteadily, doubled over, hands on our buckling knees gasp-laughing at each other, not knowing what to do with our bodies and faces – we got there, we got here, he did it.

Josh has another hour at school, we'll get him home, if I can do the school run safely while fizzing, and tell him on the sunny front lawn and it will be his turn to whoop.

We do, he does, again we yell to the skies!! Josh has to be nudged to let off steam and thinks the excitement might be too loud for the neighbours, we assure him all the neighbours all around will approve wholeheartedly. It's not an instant switch for him - we can visibly see this huge news sinking and settling, lighting him up from within. He absolutely glows. Joy-relief-gratitude. We start calling people; they shout and yell and cheer too and the phone vibrates in our hands. Let the whooping begin.

CHAPTER 28

Day 750

My middle boy, my lion cub, climbs up onto a little wooden step which lives under the bell for this purpose. He's wearing a proper shirt ("I look like Daddy!") for the occasion. The step makes me catch my breath in my throat - always the reminder that little people endure this, people little enough that they can't reach the rope on the bell. Some too small to stand on a step at all. And some never get to stand on the step. We are the lucky ones, my god we are the lucky ones.

He has copied the words of the poem onto a piece of red paper and holds it out in front of him. A small crowd has gathered around us, grandparents and cousins, hospital faces we have grown to know so well, hope-happy faces we have never seen before, consultant faces pop out of consulting doors. Albie has his hands firmly clamped over his ears and starts shouting, "Ring the bell Josh! Ring the bell Josh!"

He takes a deep breath and wiggles his left knee, then

in a little, high voice reads out:

> Ring the bell
> With all your might
> Ring the bell
> Remember your fight
> Ring the bell
> Ring your fears away
> Ring the bell
> Celebrate today

He looks across at me, questioningly, I nod with eyebrows raised, holding my breath, and he wiggles the rope. Louder Josh, louder! He clangs the bell, hard, grin-winces at the sound and laughs, everyone claps, he jumps down from the step and there is movement everywhere, bright, tears, hand shaking, noise. A hospital PR person grabs me, notepad and pen, scribbling, spread the joy, share some positive news, tell us how it feels! Everything is a bit blurry and over-bright. Everyone pops back into their place, families wait in armchairs, admin staff go back to the phones, chemo nurses return to the lounge to the beeping poles, consultants go back behind their doors. The well-oiled machine clicks seamlessly back into action.

But for us, he has rung the bell.

EPILOGUE

Now what?

I am dust motes in a sunbeam. Suspended, bathed in a gentle golden light, not falling not rising not going anywhere. I just am. I am all heart, feeling, brimming, toasty, warm, and yet I am motionless, empty. I am steeped, pickled, preserved in rich, gloopy gratitude, yet I am simultaneously numb, inert.

Now what?

The earth keeps travelling around the sun, boys grow, hair gets cut, feet get bigger, testosterone boosts. The decompression ebbs and flows. He has regular blood tests and bone marrow aspirates to see if he's staying stable and clear, which become more spaced out. The gratitude when the results are good is a physical thing; the corners of my eyes crinkle happily and stay there for hours after the phonecall (bring on the happy crow's feet, bring them on) and I am gliding, bouncing through the day.

I'm sure the gratitude does something at a cellular level,

it's a low-bubbling, weirdly internal glee in my core. From there, it radiates out around my body, it's not noisy and big and demonstrative, it's not about telling people he's still clear or sharing the news and shouting about it, it's just a spreading of goodness and contentment from the heart of me out across my shoulders and around my back and down each limb and finally out to each tiny capillary. The little voice has stopped adding 'all being well' to the end of every hope, every sentence, and dares to venture a 'yippee' from time to time. It whispers as I go about my day, "Enjoy today, enjoy today…today can be snatched from you in an instant, live now…" Do it for those who aren't so lucky. I hold them in my heart, the little faces we met along the way who didn't make it, I hold them tight, quietly ingrained for as long as my heart keeps beating. We owe it to them to live in the moment, we have to choose to master the ability to live now, to do this in memory of them.

Fast forward two years, and when Ollie is approaching his final year of primary school his teacher asks Scott and me to come in for a chat. He doesn't tell us much in advance about why, mentions some vague social dramas, and we both start to wonder if we have overlooked something major and Ollie is beginning to show some psychological effects of what we've been going through. Throughout the whole Josh journey, people have asked us how the siblings are coping. We've tried our damnedest to do the right things for them; being consistently fair, explaining when we can't be (Legomethasone), therapy milkshakes, reassurance, giving honest facts when they ask, striving for normality wherever possible, not modelling drama and panic and hysteria, keeping the boundaries of acceptable small-boy-behavior where they would have been for our family with or without leukaemia… we have tried. In some ways we have been and continue to be quite tough, being believers in the philosophy that firm rules and boundaries make young humans feel secure and loved, much as they may rally and rage against them.

So we sit down with his wonderful, young, male, inspirational, energized, slightly-magical teacher, on mini chairs, and he talks about how, as Ollie has always gravitated towards the girls for his closest friendships, he is having to learn the best ways to communicate with them now they are ten year olds and no longer very little children. The girls were in a phase of trying out how it felt to exclude each other, and, getting a bit sick of it and thinking it was all pointless and over-emotional, Ollie had called them out bluntly, as he would have done with his brothers or his male friends. We talk about ways to help him communicate with his peers depending on who they are and how they are likely to react, so that he himself doesn't become excluded from the social group. Duly baptized in tween politics, we move on to profuse thanks for all the support this teacher is giving him, and then his teacher tells us out of nowhere that he thinks Ollie should put himself forward for the election process to be a school leader (a prefect, in the UK). We look at each other, not quite sure what to say. I mean obviously we think he's great, he's our child, but we hadn't realized that his naturally calm, friendly, kind-hearted nature has apparently spread its tendrils into his school community and had an effect. At this point he isn't an alpha male, he isn't one of the fastest or the loudest or the one who shoots the most hoops. But the truth is that the teacher knows him outside our home life in a way that we don't, he sees how he interacts with those around him, deals with conflict, offers help without hesitation. So whilst we are slightly wary of getting his hopes up only for him to be disappointed, we agree to get on board, believe in him and quietly foster his confidence as he goes through the process of speeches and votes and speeches and votes...

He writes the first draft of his speech and tries it out on me and Scott, and I have to look away. It's like being hit by something physical, a plank; the language is clunky as he is only ten, but the content of the speech is really good. I mean, I have no idea what they're really looking for, but it comes straight from his heart and talks about the importance of kindness, what qualities a good leader should demonstrate and why he thinks he has them. He doesn't mention Josh or the word 'leukaemia' directly, but there is a short section where he alludes to it, saying he knows what it's like to go through tough times when you're worried about something, and he will always be there if you need a friend. My heart cracks. He does end with an unintentionally-hilarious pronouncement that 'finally, I am really, really funny' which we adapt, trying clumsily to explain that whether people find you funny is really up to them, not you, so telling them you're funny might not be the best plan.

He gets it, he's voted in as the school captain. It's announced in a ceremony where they farewell the outgoing school leaders, and we know by this point that he is one of the four boy leaders, but we don't know which role he got. And he is captain. They read out his name, his little name, in front of everyone and I burst into tears. I think it's the only time in my life that tears have kind of physically sprung out of my eyes with their own energy. I know I'm possibly making it into something bigger than it merits, but for us, for this family, this is a really big deal. For years now, I have worried that one of the three, two of the three, or, who knows, three of the three will have some level of PTSD, psychological hurdles to overcome, will it manifest itself in strange, unexpected ways, will we scratch our heads about what's going on, only to have child psychologists point out the link between the years of trauma and what's happening now? It's quite possible, probable even, that this is yet to come, we are the naïve, inexperienced parents of primary aged children, the teenage phase looms, a whole new ballgame.

So to be school captain, head boy, this feels like the universe grabbing me by the head and forcibly turning my gaze like a lighthouse beam onto the other child, after my focus has been so strongly on Josh. Look, look at THIS one now, notice him and who he is becoming! It is a strange guilt-pride, I am utterly humbled. With a massive dollop of gratitude. Much of the gratitude is directed to his incredible teacher, mentor, who believed in him and must have seen something in him that he knew he could nurture. He, the teacher, guided him over the course of the year from unassuming, kind-hearted, slightly introverted boy to someone who could stand on the stage and speak, with a flick of his hair, smiling, leading, calm, reassuring, still humble but self-assured.

Over the following year as school captain, he is often greeted by tiny children on the street in town with their parents, "Hi Ollie!" they call in their sweet, excited voices.

Ollie grins back and gives them a loud, happy, "Hi!"

"Who was that?" I ask him, "Is that your buddy?" (children in many Australian schools are given a 'buddy' from an older year to foster inclusivity and kindness across the whole school community).

Ollie, "No, no idea. The little ones all know who I am."

And I realise that while he is still little, not yet a teenager even, he is truly separate from us now, he achieved this on his own, without me, without Scott showing him every step of the way, he is becoming someone else and detaching from us. School captain wasn't something Scott or I achieved, we're not telling him what to do and how to do it. He will always be our boy, they all will, but the slow, steady journey from small child to independent adult is beginning. This is stating the obvious perhaps, but when you have been so focused on one pathway for a long time, these moments of clarity sometimes have to be right in front of your face to see them. Some mums of boys say this gradual, inexorable separating is like a slow heartbreak. I think it probably will be. But they will still be my boys, I will still squeeze their big, hairy man-hands three times in code.

I feel like my gratitude cloak which shielded me in the intensive months, swirling on a good day, cocooning on the bad, has fused into an actual part of me, been absorbed. It's definitely less magnificent now in my imagination, no longer a coat of many colours, a patchwork of textures and glinting shades, which it needed to be then to give me courage and motivation, no, now it is quiet and steady, part of the fabric of me. An undercurrent that sits below and supports everything else on top. I'm not quiet and steady though, I am a mum of three boys who are noisy and dirty and fighty and everything that three boys are.

I may now have a gratitude cloak woven into the fabric of me, but I can't claim constant zen - whenever I confiscate the laptop in a fit of rage, the red mist of the moment is so thick that I frequently have no recollection of where I end up hiding it, and spend ages the following day wandering around the house in confused bewilderment, the archetypal tragicomic mum, trying to put myself in my own angry shoes to work out where I would have hidden it. (Could we have been selectively burgled, and they only took the laptop? More likely any burglar walking into our house would assume the house had just been done by some other burglars and leave in haste.) A concerted team effort, usually aided by the boys themselves, then uncovers it somewhere utterly random like under the coatstand, or in my sock drawer.

Josh still gets all the eyelashes. Later, forever, 'Let him not relapse, ever. Whoosh…'

It's a metaphorical Tuesday morning, I'm standing in our tiny ensuite bathroom, forcing my poker straight hair into inexpert waves. I have six minutes until I need to get out of the door, before the rest of them, to work. Scott is doing the school run as he now works at home almost all the time.

(Rewind four years, psychotherapist, end of a tough session, gently, "Is there really no way Scott could find a way of working where he didn't have to stay away from the family home four nights a week?"

Me, awkwardly, "Mumble mumble not really mumble… clients face to face mumble… digital meetings not the same…mumble…"

Universe, "Here's a pandemic, try that."

Right. Gotta find those silver linings.)

Anyway, Scott is present, here in the smallest room in the house, brushing his teeth righteously because it was the right time for him to brush his teeth, while my elbows flail around my head manoeuvring the billion degree straightening tongs. Inexplicably, but obviously, the dog, a sweet-natured border collie who joined the family a year after Josh rang the bell and is the only other female in the house, is also present somewhere below me, intelligent eyes enquiring, "What are you doing, what are you doing human, what are you doing, communicate with me plz?"

Ollie: "Mu-u-um! You haven't signed my Athletics Carnival permission slip! It's due back TODAY!"

Josh: "Ollie are you doing the 1,500m? I can't decide. MU-U-UM should I do the 1,500m? I think I'll just do the discus, I like discus. MUM I wanted a lunch order why have you made me a cheese and mayo sandwich they taste like vomit? Eurgh!"

Albie, in great excitement, appearing in the bathroom doorway with arms laden with strange top-heavy Lego creations with wheels: "Mum! Mum! LOOK how many penis-cars I've made!?"

Me: ??

Scott nearly chokes on his toothbrush, snort-laughter toothpaste bubbles splat into the sink.

Josh: "Penis-cars, NICE Albs, nice! Take them in for your News day!"

Albie, hopping with excitement: "YEAH! Penis-cars for News!! Miss G will LOVE that."

Ollie: "No Albie, that is so rude and embarrassing."

Josh, dancing right up in Ollie's face: "Ollieeeeee you're so bor-ing…"

Ollie fires up, the Scorpio in him getting ready to sting, blue eyes flashing.

Albie begins handing out Lego works of art to each family member, including one for the dog who starts biting it.

Me, "Josh stop baiting Ollie! Freja (dog) – leave it! Albie you are NOT taking penis-cars in for News. Put your clothes on, how are you still half naked, brush your teeth! Library bags! Water bottles!" Etc etc.

Every. Single. Morning. But with variations on the Lego creations of course, and the intensity and escalation of the baiting. And when they get home from school, and in the car, and in the backyard, and on their bikes, and at the dinner table… they are so constant. They are so alive. All three of them.

And like that, I am blindsided on some idle Tuesday that we are out the other side.

POSTSCRIPT

If this writing has etched a little mark on any hearts and thereby encouraged more kindness, empathy and perspective in this world which sometimes feels really quite broken, then Josh's leukaemia will not have been an experience of meaningless suffering.

Yesterday is heavy. Put it down.

It is estimated that around 750 children in Australia are diagnosed with cancer every year. In the UK the figure is closer to 1,700. No child should have to endure this cruel disease. Advances in medical research are the way to improve outcomes for children with cancer. The list below is not by any means a comprehensive list of all the wonderful children's cancer charities, however these are the organisations who supported our family directly and, at times, provided us with a lifeline - medically, emotionally, financially and practically. Any donation, however modest, helps secure the future of life-saving research, and improves the quality of life for children and their families when faced with this diagnosis.

cancercentreforchildren.org.au
thekidscancerproject.org.au
campquality.org.au
redkite.org.au
kidswithcancer.org.au
starlight.org.au
RMHC.org.au

THANKS

My thanks go beaming out to so many wonderful humans; it would double the length of this little book were I to list them all by name. Thank you to every single member of the Joshie facebook group, to the dinner ladies spearheaded by Katie Falloon, the gardeners led by Kirstine McKay, to Dr Ros Bresnahan, Professor Stewart Kellie and his incredible team, to Bridget, to Donna and Mira, to the many, many 24 carat gold friends spread all around the world who sent parcels and cards and drawings, to Colleen and Hannah Matthews for creating a birthday party when I was still in shock, to the fairy godmothers Katie Dobson and Lu Scott, to Lucy Reid for her pragmatic carpark generosity, to Gill Truman for feeling like a childhood friend right from the start, to Alex Nielsen who understood, to the mental health guru that is Dr Louella Grattan-Smith, to my beautiful cousins Julie, Dick, Lizzie and Clare for their lucky charms, to my in-laws for carrying us along, and to Katie Daynes for being my sounding board and the first person to whom I dared show these vulnerable ramblings. So many, many more people are due a huge debt of gratitude and are forever carved into my grateful heart. And of course to my mum, how lucky we are to have you.

An alternative title I considered for this memoir was A Love Letter to the Medical System. Not snappy, but there it is: medics, hospital workers, first responders, support staff, every day you choose to help people. It is a choice, what we do with our lives, and your choice makes all the difference. Thank you.

Printed in Great Britain
by Amazon

42634951R00148